Ujamaa and Ubuntu

For over a decade, the world has experienced an accelerating erosion of a language that took hundreds of years to emerge. It is a language ordering time and space with words, such as enlightenment, reason, rationality, modernization, and the most recent by-word, globalization. However, it is a language that has been accompanied by colonialism, imperialism, racism, the exploitation of people and nature, an unequal distribution of the world's resources, pogroms, genocides, and world wars. There has been a gap between assumptions underlying a visionary ambition and the often-brutal practices that have accompanied it. Moreover, it is a language that expresses European values, with the implicit or explicit suggestion that they pertain to the whole world, a civilizing mission from a European centre. Although the established narrative argued that there was continuous progress, it was a conclusion reached through hindsight. The idea of progress had to be repeatedly recreated through new visionary projects that attempted to live up to the high ideals their predecessors failed to achieve.

Against the backdrop of this meta-normative point of departure, the book argues that a convincing grand narrative has failed to materialize since the discrediting of globalization. In the search for a new narrative, it argues at a meta-normative level for a reformulation of the term 'global' away from its close connection to the globe as an unbounded self-propelling market that exists beyond human influence. 'Global' should no longer be reduced to auto-playing market fiction but instead be connected to the planet, Terra, the Earth. With reference to Latour and Chakrabarty, 'global' and 'planetary' mean cohabitation; life on earth is seen as an infinite symbiotic system, nurtured, and protected, but also destroyed, by human action.

The book argues that a new conceptualization of 'the global' and 'the planet' requires input from African and Asian language cultures. The book explores in depth the history of the two political African key concepts of *ujamaa* and *ubuntu* and argues that they are cases showing how work on a new global/planetary narrative might look. The investigation of the two concepts demonstrate that translations are juxtapositions that point up what is shared and what isn't between concepts in two or more languages. The point of comparison is not to develop a uniform, global perspective, even if that were possible, but to develop a global understanding of difference and, through that, to begin to look for a common ground. Translations of political key concepts are the source of a growing understanding of difference.

Bo Stråth is professor emeritus. He was Professor of Nordic, European and World History at the Helsinki University (2007–2014), Professor of Contemporary History at the European University Institute, Florence (1997–2007), and Professor of History at the Gothenburg University (1991–1997). He is the author of *The Brandt Commission and the Multinationals. Planetary Perspectives* (Routledge, 2023), *Europe's Utopias of Peace: 1815, 1919, 1951* (2015) and co-author of *A Brief History of Political Economy* (2016) and *European Modernity: A Global Approach* (2017).

Routledge Approaches to History

52 **Combining Political History and Political Science**
   Towards a New Understanding of the Political
   Edited by Carlos Domper Lasús and Giorgia Priorelli

53 **Lebanese Historical Thought in the Eighteenth Century**
   Hayat El Eid Bualuan

54 **Polish Theory of History and Metahistory in Topolski, Pomian, and Tokarczuk**
   Jan Pomorski

55 **The Cultivation of Character and Culture in Roman Rhetorical Education**
   The Available Means
   Anthony Edward Zupancic

56 **When Jews Argue**
   Between the University and the Beit Midrash
   Edited by Ethan B. Katz, Sergey Dolgopolski and Elisha Ancselovits

57 **Historical Narratives**
   Constructable, Evaluable, Inevitable
   Mariana Imaz-Sheinbaum

58 **The Biographical Landscapes of Raphael Lemkin**
   Piotr Madajczyk

59 **Ujamaa and Ubuntu**
   Conceptual Histories for a Planetary Perspective
   Bo Stråth

For more information about this series, please visit: https://www.routledge.com/Routledge-Approaches-to-History/book-series/RSHISTHRY

Ujamaa and Ubuntu
Conceptual Histories for a Planetary Perspective

Bo Stråth

LONDON AND NEW YORK

First published 2024
by Routledge
4 Park Square, Milton Park, Abingdon, Oxon OX14 4RN

and by Routledge
605 Third Avenue, New York, NY 10158

Routledge is an imprint of the Taylor & Francis Group, an informa business

© 2024 Bo Stråth

The right of Bo Stråth to be identified as author of this work has been asserted in accordance with sections 77 and 78 of the Copyright, Designs and Patents Act 1988.

All rights reserved. No part of this book may be reprinted or reproduced or utilised in any form or by any electronic, mechanical, or other means, now known or hereafter invented, including photocopying and recording, or in any information storage or retrieval system, without permission in writing from the publishers.

Trademark notice: Product or corporate names may be trademarks or registered trademarks, and are used only for identification and explanation without intent to infringe.

British Library Cataloguing-in-Publication Data
A catalogue record for this book is available from the British Library

ISBN: 9781032641515 (hbk)
ISBN: 9781032641539 (pbk)
ISBN: 9781032641614 (ebk)

DOI: 10.4324/9781032641614

Typeset in Times New Roman
by codeMantra

Contents

Acknowledgements ix

1 **Introduction** 1
   The book's meta-normative backdrop and the subplot: the lack of a language 1
   Global translations for a planetary perspective 8
   Ujamaa and ubuntu 11

2 ***Ujamaa:*** **evasive and elusive African socialism** 17
   Nyerere and the concept of ujamaa 17
   Nyerere's speech act moment 22
   Visions of community, freedom and exploitation 28
   Visions of social justice and sacrifices made for the nation 30
   The village community: contradictions within a political program 32
   Ujamaa and development: contradictions within a concept 36
   Continuities of the colonial heritage 38
   The new master 40
   The world stage 44
   Experiences of disappointment and the philosophers 48

3 **The translation of the unwritten: *ubuntu* as religion, as law, and as politics** 56
   Ubuntu as a concept 56
   The civilizing mission and the translation of values 57
   The meaning of ubuntu in the minds of the missionaries 67
   From a concept for sin to the language of emancipation and a critique of apartheid 75
   Post-apartheid: ubuntu for reconciliation 79

*The anti-neoliberal defiance and the new politics
of social distribution* 83
Reconciliation glossed over 86

Epilogue: can we learn from *ujamaa* and *ubuntu*? 94

Index 103

Acknowledgements

My work on the conceptual history of *ujamaa* and *ubuntu* was made possible through serial fellowships at the Stellenbosch Institute for Advanced Studies (STIAS). I am most grateful to Hendrik Geyer, the then director of STIAS, but my thanks also extend to his perennially helpful staff. The intellectual environment that they created was full of generosity, creativity, and stimulation. The staff at the university library in Stellenbosch provided me with an excellent loan and interlibrary service. The talks with John Noyes, Tony Hopkins, and Richard Price among the STIAS fellows gave me many ideas. My thanks also go to Sam Sadian who edited the texts in a first version.

The origin of this short book was a research project initiated at Helsinki University in 2008 that aimed to contribute to a new kind of world history – conceptual history as world history – as opposed to the globalization narrative that, at the time, was hegemonic and which that year reached its zenith. The focus of the project was on the conceptualization of the social and economic in Eurasian and Eurafrican languages and translations. Henrik Stenius, the then director of the Centre of Nordic Studies, gave me great support by personally committing his Centre to this new direction of connecting Norden to a larger European and global context, for which I thank him warmly. The project became soon a joint venture with Hagen Schulz-Forberg at the Århus University. The cooperation brought important methodological and theoretical incentives. Dipesh Chakrabarty was from early on a committed participant in the conferences, workshops, and project meetings. His *Provincializing Europe* was a source of inspiration at the outset. More recently I have derived my planetary perspective from his book *The Climate of History in a Planetary Age* and its follow-up *One Planet, Many Worlds*.

The core of the *ujamaa* chapter comes from a text called 'Ujamaa – the Evasive Translation of an Elusive Concept' which was published in a 2016 volume of collected articles, '*Doing Conceptual History in Africa*' (Axel Fleisch and Rhiannon Stephens (eds), New York and Oxford: Berghahn, 2016: pp 185–212). The text has been thoroughly revised, updated, and amended to sit better alongside the *ubuntu* chapter and match the overall normative theme of this short book, i.e., the planetary perspective, which, since then, has considerably developed. I didn't think of the term planetary at that time. I am grateful to Andreas Eckert for his crucial comments, Rhiannon Stephens for help with the Swahili-to-English translations and Axel Fleisch for our etymological discussions and his general remarks and suggestions. I am most grateful to John Wakota for reading and commenting on the revised version and assisting with search for illustrations. On this latter point, I also want to thank Dominicus Makukula very much.

In terms of the *ubuntu* chapter, I would like to express my warmest thanks to Tom Bennett for all our discussions on the *ubuntu* concept, and to Christian Gade who gave me access to some of his source texts which, together with his own writing on *ubuntu*, has been of great assistance. Ntozakhe Cezula played an invaluable part with his English translation of the use of *ubuntu* in the 1846 Xhosa version of the New Testament and for information about the work of missionaries in nineteenth-century South Africa. On this latter point, I am also grateful for the help of Dion Forster and Retief Muller. Jacob Moikanyang assisted me by providing translation from Tswana, which proved crucial. Rieke Jordan was a great help with the illustrations for the *ubuntu* chapter and Johan Stråth with those for the *ujamaa* chapter. Rieke also formatted the end notes and the references and made the index. Finally, many thanks to Tim Luscombe for his help with the language wash in the introduction and the epilogue and the sections of new text in the *ujamaa* and *ubuntu* chapters. My last but not least thanks go to Angela who, as always, always was there.

Rhodt, October 2023
Bo Stråth

1 Introduction

The book's meta-normative backdrop and the subplot: the lack of a language
Global translations for a planetary perspective
Ujamaa and ubuntu

The book's meta-normative backdrop and the subplot: the lack of a language

For over a decade, the world has experienced an accelerating erosion of a language that took hundreds of years to emerge. It is a language ordering time and space with words, such as enlightenment, reason, rationality, modernization, and the most recent by-word, globalization. However, it is a language that has been accompanied by colonialism, imperialism, racism, the exploitation of people and nature, an unequal distribution of the world's resources, pogroms, genocides, and world wars. There has been a gap between assumptions underlying a visionary ambition and the often-brutal practices that have accompanied it. Moreover, it is a language that expresses European values, with the implicit or explicit suggestion that they pertain to the whole world; a civilizing mission from a European centre.

Although the established narrative argued that there was continuous progress, it was a conclusion reached through hindsight. The idea of progress had to be repeatedly recreated through new visionary projects that attempted to live up to the high ideals their predecessors failed to achieve.

Today, however, no new vision of enlightenment and progress seems to be emerging. The tension between ideal and practice seems to have become overstretched. The historical capacity to rise above dread and disaster and create new, mobilizing hope seems to be lost. The knack of facing the future by learning processes, translating experiences of disappointment into new expectations, seems harder to master. The language of modernization – with its origin in the several centuries-old processes of industrialization, democratization, colonialism, and imperialism, culminating in the globalization tale – has lost its capacity to convince.

The world cries out for a language that can come to terms with and somehow help resolve today's entangled issues – the exhaustion of resources, the existential climate catastrophe, mass migrations in the wake of droughts, floods, famines and wars, cultures of hospitality becoming cultures of hostility, and the current attempt to create a new world order focusing on the world's nations, ever less united, and their strongmen leaders under the demonization of the Other. Authoritarian governments prosper by exploiting resignation and nurturing old-school nationalism and racism, which of course are no less incendiary than they were a century ago. Nationalism underpins the emergence of hostile geopolitical blocks transferring nationalism to a global scale of geopolitical hostility. It is no longer the bipolar world of the Cold War but something more fateful than the euphonious term multipolar suggests. Fateful because the pattern recalls historical catastrophes.

From this gloomy scenario of the world's ills, one conclusion is obvious – that there is an urgent need for a new orientation – something radically different from the attempt to look for the future in a nationalistic and xenophobic past. A new orientation means a new interpretative framework based on a new conceptualization. The peoples of the world must respond to the entangled challenges they face by building a global culture that connects local, regional, and planetary perspectives in new ways. The challenge is to find a language for a new economic order that encompasses ecology, that protects and nurtures rather than squanders scarce resources, and distributes their yield fairly. The challenge is to find a language that promotes our peaceful cohabitation by transforming hard borders into soft boundaries, demarcations into 'overlappings' and hostility into hospitality, and that pays attention to the distinction between hospitality as guest and inhabitant. In one of his last interviews, Bruno Latour said that the world urgently needs a new Copernican Revolution to create a language of understanding, not about the relationship between the Earth and the Sun, but about our life and earthly cohabitation in which we humans are not the only inhabitants. A key question is how any new conceptualization incorporates the new historical-geological era of the Anthropocene. The task is daunting.

Immanuel Wallerstein distinguished between modernization and modernity, the former being the supposed human triumph over nature through the promotion of technological innovations, the latter being the triumph of humankind over itself, an emancipation from oppression and economic servitude.[1] Beginning with the Bandung conference in 1955 and with a first culmination with the Third World claims for a New International Economic Order in the 1970s, the imaginary of emancipation widened from a European/Western concern to a global struggle for more justice and a fairer distribution of the Earth's resources. Aimé Césaire wrote at the time of Bandung about a project of Europeanization of the world without European domination.[2] The tail end of this discourse was Dipesh Chakrabarty's *Provincializing Europe* in 2001. The growth of the middle classes in China, India, and elsewhere outside the West under the motto of eliminating mass poverty, the desirable triumph of modernity at a global level clashed with the modernization goal of the technological triumph over nature. The growing warnings since the 1970s of exhaustion of natural resources, environmental pollution and at the end the climate crisis, suggests that technological capacity is not unbounded as Wallerstein might have believed. The Club of Rome Report *Limits to Growth* in 1972 about global resource exhaustion threw its long shadow over the 1970s. The vision of (Western) technology triumph over nature lost credibility. The emancipative modernity approach at a global level, the other strand of Wallerstein's thought, has ended in a crisis as Bruno Latour and Dipesh Chakrabarty conclude.[3] The growing insights that earth's resources are limited weakened Wallerstein's modernity model. With declining resources and growing environment and climate problems, the scope for redistribution erodes, or better put, becomes a zero-sum game of giving and taking rather than giving to all through sustainable growth. The climate and environmental crisis hits both of Wallerstein's categories in their entanglements. Justified claims for a larger share of the pie clash with considerations of the global redistribution of scarce resources and the yields of their exploitation.

One might against this gloomy backdrop describe today's crisis as a lack of a language, a lack of a narrative that inspires and promotes action against the climate deterioration and the soil and resource exhaustion for our peaceful cohabitation on Earth appealing to human responsibility, a language of the type Latour demanded. Instead, what is emerging is a new language that leads our minds in the opposite direction, towards authoritarianism, xenophobic nationalism, and racism. A military project for the resurrection of the Soviet Union in the incarnation of a Russian empire 2.0 adds fuel to the chaotic situation and the martial mood. While the war has a unifying impact on the West, the Global South comment on it with an impassive shrug of the shoulders mixed with a cynicism engendered by their memories of the Cold War when many proxy wars were fought in the South. This cynicism stands in the way of reconciliation, but the question is on what historical grounds it can be overcome.

It is escapism when commentators in the West believe that colonialism is the ground for the indifference in the Global South, because the colonial experiences are seen as historical facts generations away without personal responsibilities or feelings of guilt. In that sense, they are a historical abstraction in the North. In the South much less so, since colonialism is seen as a historical continuity to the present-day North-South situation. Decolonisation is considered much less of a rupture in the South than in the West. However, the Cold War memories of proxy warfare in the South is a much more relevant factor for the weak preparedness to condemn Russia. The lack of readiness in this respect should not be misunderstood as a general support of Russia or of not seeing the neo-imperial dimension of the war on Ukraine, however.

It is difficult not to hear a similar indifference concerning support for the Western condemnation of the Hamas mass massacre on civilian Israelis during the proofreading of this book. The two frontlines of Western culture are connected and reinforce the cementation of new hostile geopolitical blocks just referred to. The comments from the South ask, explicitly or implicitly, where the West was when similar things happened in Sudan, Congo, and many other places. It is not that they all agree with Russia or Hamas, but they condemn the West's selective and self-centred attention, which can be labelled hypocrisy. One might see the Hamas horrific outrage and mass murder as a new earthquake along the old rift between the West and the rest. Many in the South consider Israel itself responsible for the terrible violence it is facing even if they on principle condemn it. The foundation of the state of Israel as a compensation for the genocidal attempt by a European state to extinguish all Jews at the sacrifice of the Palestine population was never seriously questioned in the West – to deep was the Holocaust shock – and it was silently accepted in large parts of the rest of the world. The opposition grew when Israel developed to a settler-colonial state after the Six-Day War in 1967 ignoring the UN Resolution 446 in 1979 on West Jordania, Gaza, and Golan. The Western condemnation of Russia with reference to international law and the West's unwillingness to see and condemn the Israel ignorance of international law is a contradiction and hypocrisy. Hypocrisy connects the Russia-Ukraine and the Israel-Palestine crises.

Against this backdrop, another relevant factor behind the lack of general commitment in the struggle against the West's problems is the fortress reaction to the growing number of economic and climate refugees. The fortress reactions mean the reinterpretation of the asylum rules, and the redefinition of the subjects of protection from the refugees to the Western countries themselves who see the migrants as intruders. These recent developments and the hypocrisy that accompany them prevent reconciliation with the South and a unison planetary condemnation of an imperial war and mass slaughter of civilian populations. The problem is less faults and offences in the past than in the present. The problem is the hypocrisy that drives the reactions to the world crisis in the West. Here one might recall Reinhart Koselleck's warning that hypocrisy paves the way towards the hypocrisis, the (hypo)crisis as the negation of hypocrisy.[4] More self-critical reflection, scepticism, and political imagination and fantasy would be mental instruments against hypocrisy and the (hypo)crisis.

The globalization narrative lost legitimacy in the wake of the 2008 financial collapse. It described a world of market auto-play, with democracy subjugated to the markets' requirements, whoever determined those requirements. It was argued that what the market required was 'without alternatives,' and democracies needed to be market compliant. Three decades of this market discourse have played down the role of human agency and human responsibility in historical processes. Bottom-up redistribution, from the poor to the rich, from labour to capital, worldwide, became self-evident, a matter of course. Without really questioning it, humans had been brought under the control of an anonymous force called the Market, which, it was argued, orders the world more rationally than anything else. Until 2008, the Market was boundless and infinite. Few believe in that tale anymore. The alternative that emerges in protests against the neoliberal ravages is authoritarian nationalism. It is an emotional reaction of fury against the "cosmopolitans," whoever they are, argued to be the executors of the globalization.

We still live in the shadow of the collapse of discursive power that took place in 2008. Appeals to action against the climate change remain in many respects a moral meta narrative without a strong personal action imperative. Rather than a general mobilization of the opinions for a struggle against the climate crisis, polarizing and clashing languages for or against climate discourse emerge.

What in the 1980s came to be called the linguistic turn, saw a major epistemological shift from the conventional perspective, prevalent since Plato's time, that separated the 'real' from the world of ideas, and materialism from idealism. In the emergent view in the 1980s, language not only reflects the world but constitutes it. What we cannot express through our concepts, we cannot know. We describe, analyze, explore, and discover 'reality' by conceptualizing it. Physics, by means of a continuous flow of increasingly refined concepts, maps and describes ever-deeper insights into the microcosmos of an atom as well as the macrocosmos of a solar system. This is arguably also applicable for mapping and describing life on Earth, life not only in a biological, but also in a cultural and historical sense.

The meta-normative argument set out here is that there is a need for a new language that constitutes a new reality, a new world beyond our current conceptualization of the chaotically entangled issues of climate catastrophe, racism, and xenophobic nationalism. The pacifying globalization narrative is dead and there is no need to regret its loss. Instead, there is a need for a new counter-narrative that embraces a global effort to engage people in a new ordering of life on Earth, one that is more peaceful and has a fairer distribution of resources, and one that reflects on the recently coined term Anthropocene.

The task is a redefinition of the meaning of 'the global,' one that will render it distinct from the globalization narrative and globalism that followed in its wake. 'Global' can no longer be reduced to market fiction but should be connected to the planet ('Terra,' 'the Earth') as seen from space. 'Planetary,' in turn, must be distinguished from its astronomical connotation of a dot in an endless universe. Planetary must mean the Earth as seen from orbiting satellites ever since the launch of Sputnik in 1957. The Earth, viewed from space, is finite but borderless. The satellites' optic equipment discerns continents and oceans. From this viewpoint, the traces humans have left on Earth during their present, brief geological era, the Anthropocene, are also visible. The view discerns vegetation and perceives life on earth as an endless symbiotic system, infinitely complex and therefore also fragile and vulnerable. The view discerns how, on Earth, macrocosmos meets microcosmos, a meeting that provokes questions about planetary cohabitation and human responsibility as well as action for the maintenance of the symbiotic system itself.

The concept of the Anthropocene is at odds with the globalization narrative. Anthropocene focuses our attention on man's impact on the world, seeing it as a quasi-geological force, though one which acts much faster than any natural agent can transform land masses and oceans. Man can destroy them. The term 'Anthropocene' is a correction and an objection to the dream of the globe as an unbounded market with endless resources, a dream that in a Freudian sense represses the term 'exploitation' (either of nature or of humans). One can only conclude that, in order to lead our action and vision for the world in new directions, globalization, and everything that concept came to stand for, must be replaced by a new conceptualization with the idea of 'global' in a planetary perspective at its heart.

The discourse around globalization was a strong expression of the nineteenth-century Eurocentric narrative in which capitalism and democracy, as ever-expanding forces in mutually reinforcing dynamics, civilized and modernized the world from its European centre. The launch of Sputnik in 1957 introduced a new phase in the story of European human progress. The Soviet Union's hubris was matched by the USA's fears of losing the space race. Hannah Arendt cut through the contentious Cold War perspectives, seeing the event from an Earth-human one, as an extension of man's half-a-millennium-old ambition to discover the world. Since around 1500, the circumnavigators explored the world, and when they had mapped it, they foresaw space exploration and cherished the dream of escaping Earth once it had been fully explored. This goal contained the danger of Earth alienation, Arendt wrote – perilous because the Earth-bound nature of humans was impossible to disentangle from their human condition. Arendt's notion of Earth alienation hinted at the risk of humanity's destruction of itself.[5] In the same sombre vein, Reinhart Koselleck found that "our globe... has become a closed spaceship" roving in an endless universe.[6]

Arendt was far from alone in her warning of earth alienation and Koselleck was not the only one who shared her concerns. Already in 1956, the year before Sputnik, Harry Martinsson published his verse poem *Aniara* about the space transporter with 8000 emigrants from the Earth bound for March, escaping environment pollution and wars, clashing with meteorites and getting off course, but defying them continuing towards what had no end.

Arendt's focus was on all technological development since 1500 rather than man's more recent interest in space. Her concern was the technological development that had led to man's ability to escape the Earth's atmosphere. Her 1950s warning of technological hubris was connected to a long tradition of warnings about the destructive risks of the machine age, Nietzsche being one of the strongest voices in that chorus. Today Arendt's warning is reflected in our current fears about the transcendence of the human embodiment of reason into artificial intelligence. Who makes up the forces which programme AI? Who controls AI and who is it controlling? Who assumes the moral authority to replace Kant with anonymous algorithms?

Dipesh Chakrabarty comments on Arendt's concern in his development of a planetary perspective on life on Earth. Arendt's view, he argues, leaves humans with two alternatives: to feel homeless (referring to her notion of Earth alienation) or to work towards what he calls a planetary unity in which all humans come to identify with the planet as their home and, by implication, transcend racial, ethnic, religious, and class boundaries.[7] Chakrabarty's second option offers an alternative to Arendt's fear of Earth alienation, and to Koselleck's, Martinsson's, and many others' dystopian views. His scenario, a counter-image of hope and possibilities, is a response to their warnings. It is a counter-image in which people identify with the planet as their home, and it makes points similar to those in Achille Mbembe's work on the conceptualization of hospitality and hostility.[8]

Chakrabarty's invitation to the world's human inhabitants to "work on" planetary unity distinguishes that unity from utopian historical projects about final world unity, which are teleological and self-propelling towards a final goal inherent in the historical process itself, such as liberal market globalization, its Marxist counter-story, or other similar mystifications. To "work on..." implies hard work, facing and coming to terms with disagreements about how to shape the future and within the context of difficult discursive disputes, where nothing is predetermined. It is strenuous work by humans, with humans being responsible for their success or failure and their destiny. Human agency and responsibility, rather than beliefs in goal-bound automatic processes intrinsic in history itself, are appealed to. There is no History – singular, and with a capital H – whether it's called Liberalism, Socialism, Nationalism, the End of History, or anything else. For good or evil, there are only human-made histories – in the plural.[9]

The planetary perspective in this book connects to and develops the planetary perspective outlined in my recent book about Willy Brandt's North/South commission.[10] Both books draw on Chakrabarty's outline of a planetary perspective.

Chakrabarty's *One Planet, Many Worlds* (2023) is a short book with three lectures given in 2017, thus four years before *The Climate of History in a Planetary Age* but updated to respond to critique in the debate on the latter book. It is thus both a presage and a follow-up. Chakrabarty expands in the short book on the distinction between the planet as natural history, which focuses on the geological period of the Anthropocene with humankind as a geological force, and the human-made histories in the plural based on human agency. The former refers to the planet, the latter to the many worlds. One might see the distinction as a development of Wallerstein's contrast between modernization and modernity, a contrast between entities that were and are entangled, but updated and reconceptualized problematizing Wallerstein's belief in progress. Anthropocene means an accelerating human impact as a geological force, the development of the planet by geobios powers. However, it is a different human impact than the human agency in the many worlds with many histories struggling to come to terms with poverty and famine, inequalities and human distress and destitution, part of which is a spillover from long-term processes in the natural history of the Anthropocene, increasingly and acceleratingly human-made with short-term implications. Wallerstein's conceptualization describes a virtuous circle whereas Chakrabarty tries to come to terms with a vicious circle. Two kinds of zeitgeist explain the difference.[11] The relative optimism about finding solutions and coming to terms with the world's ills in the 1970s has in the 2020s become scepticism and pessimism. The issue at stake is the connection between the many worlds and the one planet, the capacity of the strife in the many worlds without any superior ordering master mind to nevertheless mobilize and coordinate forces for a common struggle against the negative impact of humankind as a geological force. What Wallerstein saw as the prospects of a virtuous circle between modernization and modernity has become a vicious circle between the human power as a geological force and the human struggle in the many worlds for a better future, where the definition of better is highly contentious. The key to turn the vicious circle is what according to Latour requires a Copernican conceptual revolution.

Césaire and Chakrabarty have laid a foundation stone for this Sisyphean task. In *Provincializing Europe*, Chakrabarty argued that, though the idea that enlightenment and reason, in providing a criticism of and a corrective to the world's ills, might have a European origin, the use of such instruments of development was available beyond Europe, and even *against* Europe as the source of colonialism and imperialism. The European values that underlay critical reason became universal by provincializing their European origin.[12] Europe became only one part of a world that applied its values.

Provincializing Europe called for an end to the idea that Westernization equates to universalism. The provincialization of Europe has also meant the universalization of Europe, but it was a universalization of European values that no longer comes from within, but from without. Furthermore, as European values lost their European centre, what had been panegyric-confirming became critical-questioning. The achievement remains, and complaining conservatives, who take external criticism of the West personally and see recognition of it as unnecessary self-flagellation, form an increasingly weak rearguard. This argument connects to what was said about hypocrisy above. The final expression of the West's version 'from within' which claimed universal applicability was globalization. The future should be about a version 'from without.'

So far, this introductory chapter has described a meta-normative backdrop outlining a subplot for the pages that follow and hinting at the book's aim, which is to argue for work on a new conceptualization that will lead to a new planetary understanding of the global. However, that goal is not a teleological one constructed inside capital-H-History but a human-made one that continues the contentious work of shaping the future and will be continually revised to fit with Chakrabarty's alternative to Hannah Arendt's warning of Earth alienation. Chakrabarty's proposal about feeling at home on the planet – set against Arendt's dystopia – should not be seen as a new world emerging from an apocalypse, or a transcendence towards perfection, but, instead, as an ideal type, in Max Weber's sense, one to which we can measure the remaining distance in the attempt to approach it, progresses as well as reverses. The intellectual point of reference is not to Hegel, but to Kant and his mantra about the need for permanent progress without ever arriving at a final goal. The meta-norm is about promoting action in a Kantian way, action guided by ideas of a planetary future confronting the presentism that followed with the globalization tale where the dreams of an unbounded market and consumption in the present made the future collapse. Action towards a human-made planetary future like the one Chakrabarty proposes.[13] Action of a different kind than the raw and impulsive *re*action guided by backward-looking nostalgy about a past that should have been gone but is coming back.

The rest of the Introduction will provide more focus to this normative backdrop, formulate the intent of the book more precisely, and introduce the following chapters.

Global translations for a planetary perspective

The old Western narrative about enlightenment, development, modernization, and globalization was based on Western concepts such as freedom, human rights, and democracy, along with the belief in their universality. Arguably, a new global narrative should make non-European concepts more prominent. One might imagine the construction of a kind of global universalism with a conceptualization made from the bricks of many different languages. However, the aim is not a shared language such as Esperanto, or even English, though it functions as the world's lingua franca. This short book proposes the use of concepts from several language cultures to constitute a global interpretative framework and an arena for debate. This arrangement would obviously involve translations between languages, translations for new understandings. It underpins and illustrates the proposal with the two case studies of *ujamaa* and *ubuntu*.

The founder of a new approach to conceptual history, Reinhart Koselleck, with his arguments entrenched in European, and especially German empiricism, once referred to the concept of *citoyen*, the word that so helped mobilize people for the French revolution. He noticed that, while in English, the word would be translated as 'citizen' (almost the same but with a very different connotation), in German it would become *Staatsbürger*. Whereas *citoyen* refers to an emancipated individual who, through revolution, took destiny into his or her own hands and established a political order that defied repression and exploitation, *Staatsbürger* refers to a subject working obediently within the state and under its ruler, quite a different animal from the *citoyen*. Different words had emerged from different histories, and young Koselleck's conclusion was that the conceptual difference was too large to allow for useful comparison.

Later, he came to the opposite conclusion when he realized that difference could bring analytical strength. What, he asked, was the difference between the concepts, and what were the similarities? The questions prompted a comparative study of political cultures. Different concepts revealed different historical developments while attempting to define identical phenomena. They stood for both distinction and overlap. Taken together, they connected a variety of historical experiences and the various solutions to shared phenomena.

Walter Benjamin drew attention to the limits – and the potential – of translations. The original is not available for the reader, he argued. Translation is an art, not a transmission of linguistic content. It is something that builds a capacity for imitation. Benjamin did not despair because of this insight. Rather, he pointed out that mimesis, the principle of imitation, is a source of richness.[14]

Benjamin's argument and Koselleck's example demonstrate that there is no precise translation between any two languages. Translations are juxtapositions that point up what is shared and what isnt. Translations have the potential to promote understandings of difference and of the Other, which, in turn, encourage new perspectives on the Self. Translations are a key instrument for the development of a global approach to understanding difference and, on that basis, they promote questions about what is shared, and about how the different experiences expressed in various concepts can underpin the search for common ground based on understanding and accepting difference. Shared experiences do not necessarily mean shared interpretations of them but understanding the Other's interpretations even while disagreeing.

The point of comparison is not to develop a uniform, global perspective, even if that were possible, but to develop a global understanding of difference and, through that, begin to look to a common future that draws on the knowledge that we are all different from each other.

In the 1970s, Koselleck's conceptual history, *Begriffsgeschichte*, was undervalued and marginalized, but subsequently, conceptual history has established itself in academia. We now see that the linguistic turn in the 1980s was an epistemological landslide that forced language and its concepts into the very centre of the Humanities. With the exploration of politically mobilizing concepts, and of how they were used to appropriate interpretative priority, new understandings of historical processes emerged. With conceptual history, an exploration of change became a matter of language and interpretation. Who had the power to give meaning to or interpret phenomena? What concepts lead to political and economic strength? Who had the power to define a problem and find its solution by redefining old concepts or inventing new ones? Conceptual battles played out through contested interpretations of political and economic power.

A new world history for a new understanding of life (in a biological, social, and cultural sense) and of our cohabitation on earth, must integrate perspectives understood through discourse in non-Western cultures. The optimal methodology to establish such an alternative world history would focus on social, economic, political, religious, and cultural fields, as well as a semantic understanding around them that would be reached through a comparative study of various languages, rather than by prioritizing one (Western) one.[15]

The argument here is that conceptual history provides a key for the development of a global understanding in a planetary perspective of what, despite our different experiences and interpretations of them, might be shared across language cultures, and for an increased understanding of the historical grounds of differences. Such a global understanding would be the point of departure for the elaboration of the planetary perspective that Chakrabarty and Mbembe propose. The exploration in this short book of the emergence of two discourses around two key concepts – *ujamaa* in Tanzania and *ubuntu* in South Africa – is meant as an illustration of the argument. The exploration shows that successful concepts are often close to failure or, indeed, fail, and that we might learn more from the failures than the triumphs.

In the end, the task is to come to terms with the North/South issue and transcend the polarity. Looking backwards, one might describe phases of North/South relations during the last three-quarters of a century as follows: (1) The development and decolonization discourse in the 1950s and 1960s, including the belief that, in terms of modernization and modernity, the South would catch up with the North through development aid and self-help. (2) The dependence and neocolonialism discourse in the 1960s and 1970s, which argued that the North wasn't helping the South but, instead, the growing wealth in the North was built on the exploitation of the South. The South developed the North and thus remained poor. This phase culminated in the 1970s when the South, then known as the Third World, claimed a New International Economic Order (NIEO) and assigned a new role for the United Nations. (3) In the 1970s and 1980s, the North fended off the South's claims, arguing that all countries were partners in a market, and that the countries of the South were responsible for their own development. This would occur through market opening. (4) Instead, market opening flooded the Southern markets with cheap agricultural and industrial goods and continued the exploitation of their raw materials. (5) The present, in which waves of refugees escape political persecution, economic destitution and environmental deterioration by risking their lives in search of the

North's protection. The Northern governments, reacting to populist pressures, confront the migrants with their redefinition of protection: the object of protection is no longer the poor migrants and refugees but themselves. They abandon established asylum rules and develop often brutal anti-immigration policies. Development aid is rechannelled towards unscrupulous dictators and military regimes on the proviso that they will prevent the movement of migrants and help the North protect its fortress. Why couldn't that money be used instead on cooperation projects focusing on green energy and environmental protection, making it possible to develop living conditions in the South and thus reduce the need for migration in the first place?

Ujamaa and ubuntu

Ujamaa became a catchword that fired imaginations in the young state of Tanzania when, at the beginning of February 1967, in a charismatic speech in Dar es Salem, the country's president, Julius Nyerere, proclaimed that Tanzania would become an *ujamaa* nation based on self-reliance. He spoke to one hundred thousand enthusiastic people of a declaration that the TANU (The Tanganyika African National Union), the country's only political party, had adopted in Arusha a week before. His outline of the future was inspired by British social-democratic Fabianism and Chinese Maoist communism and was accompanied by the ambition of translating them into an African experience or, perhaps better phrased, giving them an African origin.

The speech on the Arusha Declaration was galvanizing, charismatic and visionary, later achieving an iconic reputation. It was inspired and enlivened by Western thought, though Nyerere framed it in a determinedly Tanzanian context: socialism without class struggle, modernity through agrarian village and farm-labourer communities, democracy with only one political party. The speech on the Arusha Declaration was a performative speech act ('to say something is to do something'); a moment of clarity when certain Swahili concepts were loaded with new visions.[16]

Ujamaa was a concept intended to inspire Tanzanians to become self-reliant and think of themselves as a united people. The country was a nation of agricultural workers, a village community. *Ujamaa* has traditionally been equated with 'African socialism,' but this represents an attempt to define and classify the term rather than translate it. It exposes the Western and Chinese aspects rather than the wished-for African roots.

Ujamaa is an Arabic concept, meaning to collect or to gather, and it hints at some kind of community or collection of people. In Swahili, the term *juma* means Friday, connoting Friday prayer and religious community. *Ujamaa's* political meaning in Nyerere's speech referred to the village community, the backbone of the economy and the social life in Tanzania.

Ujamaa started out more closely resembling the sort of social democracy that Nyerere had come to know during his student years in Britain, reformist with a Fabian touch of slow, gradual change. However, in the political implementation of the declaration, key sectors of the economy were immediately nationalized, a step which hardly connoted Fabianism. Also, the further development of the *ujamaa* discourse illustrates the contradictions and ambiguities of decolonization and post-colonialism. The next chapter will show how the concept lost its mobilizing power in the 1970s when the insight emerged that decolonization did not automatically mean development. It will show how the happy partners of development and democracy, or capitalism and democracy, are often in fact opposites and even incompatible. Indeed, *ujamaa* makes an interesting case study for conceptual historical analysis.

Ubuntu became a key concept in the South African break from Apartheid in the 1990s. *Ubuntu* is Ngumi, the language most spoken at home in southern Africa. *Ubu-* is a prefix forming abstract noun and *ntu* means person or human being, so *ubuntu* connotes humankind, humanism, and humanity. In building a new South Africa after Apartheid, the concept helped bring about reconciliation and construct a new community. Chapter 3 outlines the long conceptual history of the term, beginning with Christian missionaries in the 1820s and 1830s who were looking for words in the spoken but unwritten indigenous languages in order to disseminate their gospel to those with quite different religious awareness and views often in conflict with the Bible's message. The missionaries looked for something in the locally used idioms in search of language to describe abstractions that didn't exist in the indigenous peoples' minds, their task was made harder when they tried to write down what were exclusively spoken languages. It was a delicate, risky task, and they trod tentatively, as the chapter will show. It also describes the slow process of the secularization and politicization of *ubuntu* that occurred through the twentieth century, paving the way for its mushrooming in the 1990s when it influenced not only political but also legal thought in South Africa. Politicization meant, among other things, that the original universalism associated with *ubuntu* shifted towards Africanism, becoming a term that argued for African humanism based on an African philosophy with African values from a worldview centred on Africa. On this point, it is interesting to connect the history of *ubuntu* as a concept with the translation of *ujamaa* as 'African socialism.' The chapter shows that there exists a similar ambiguity and openness to interpretations in *ubuntu* as in *ujamaa*, making it a good illustration of the potential for conceptual history to create new global understandings of difference and planetary perspectives. The comparison in the following chapters will show that *ujamaa* and *ubuntu* are more than two parallel semantics. The two concepts are deeply connected. *Ubuntu* in Ngumi is *utu* in Swahili, and *utu* was at the core of the *ujamaa* discourse. *Ubuntu's* and *utu's* common concern is the definition of being a human in relation to other humans. The context of and relation to other humans define humans. They share an idea of the community of humankind, and this pattern is also visible in other African language cultures. Seen through this African perspective, the West's focus since the Renaissance and the Enlightenment has been on the individual, while the community or society are defined from the perspective of the individual. In one case, the community forms the individual, in the other, the individuals form the community. True, this view of the West is restricted to the liberal West. Marx and his many adherents attacked this focus on the individual and replaced it with a focus on collective social forms such as 'bourgeoisie' and 'working class.' But his class struggle was far from the values that the *ujamaa* and *ubuntu* semantics conveyed. On this point, it is interesting to connect to the philosophy of Hannah Arendt whose definition of freedom was different from the standard liberal emphasis on individual freedom. She insisted that freedom is shared and public, as opposed to individual and private. Freedom is characteristic of public rather than private life. Human communities are sites for freedom as well as spaces to be used to build common institutions for public life, lawgiving and imagining a better world.[17] In other words, Arendt comes close to *ubuntu's* and *utu's* outline of the human condition, and her appeal to human responsibility and human agency is far from the idea, for example, of class consciousness as an inherent force in the historical process.

Neither *ubuntu* nor *utu* convey any transcendence in their view on the future. If there is a religious dimension, and there is, it is more a moral and ethical appeal for human cohabitation. There is less goal-bound orientation and teleology than in European philosophy and Christian religion. From this pattern, it follows that in African secularized politics there are few revolutionary ideas, with or without a cleansing apocalypse before utopia can be realized dividing the existing world from the future post-apocalypse world. In concepts like *ubuntu* and *utu*, there is, in fact, less transcendental utopian thinking to do with shaping the future, but that's not to say that, within the concepts, there are no visions, dreams or expectations about the future.

On this point, it is important to emphasize that this book does not suggest the African model, archaic or not, is superior to any European or Western version. The fact that there might be more consensual thought in the African philosophy does not mean that there are no conflicts, and it is also true that not all those conflicts were triggered by interaction with the colonialists. The critical dimension of the European Enlightenment heritage is a resource beyond Europe, as Chakrabarty in *Provincializing Europe* argues. Instead of outlining an African and a European model, both utopian, the question is what could be learnt from each to benefit the development of a planetary perspective as defined at the beginning of the chapter.

How can the African experience (which translates into a new perspective on the world) meet with its European equivalent? What institutions would the negotiation of different experiences require? Could a reformed United Nations, with an emphasis on *United* rather than Nations, as in its original creation, become the institutional centre of a new normative world order that replaces international law and its Western and colonial historical bias?[18] A reformed United Nations, looking for a new identity, might recall the dynamic mid-1970s when the G77 and the Third World made the UN the centre of their expectations in an NIEO.[19]

These questions are beyond the scope of this short book, but its aim is to provoke an interest in them and similar questions about what a new world order might look like, prompting visions and expectations, hopefully without utopian overreach. The African thinking that the book evinces and wishes to promote is, as stated above, connected to European political thought, though Kantian rather than Hegelian; Kantian in the sense of constant work towards a better world, with the knowledge that one will never reach an ideal situation but might be pragmatically guided by the idea of it. The book shows how that road is bordered with failures and concludes with the argument that giving up is a less good option than learning from one's mistakes and making better decisions in the future.

Notes

1 Quoted from Dipesh Chakrabarty, *One Planet, Many Worlds. The Climate Parallax*. Waltham: Mass: Brandeis University Press, 2023: 53
2 Aimé Césaire, *Discourse on Capitalism*, transl Joan Pinkham. New York: Monthly Review, 1972: 24–25 (French original *Discours sur le capitalisme* 1955. Quoted from Chakrabarty, *One Planet* 54.
3 Bruno Latour and Dipesh Chakrabarty, "Conflicts of Planetary Proportions," *Journal of Philosophy of History*, 14, no. 3 (2020).
4 Reinhart Koselleck, *Kritik und Krise. Eine Studie zur Pathogenese der bürgerlichen Welt* (Frankfurt am Main: Suhrkamp, 1973 [1959]). Engl. transl. *Critique and Crisis: Enlightenment and the Pathogenesis of Modern Society*. Oxford: Berg, 1988.
5 Hannah Arendt, *The Human Condition* (Chicago: Chicago University Press, 1958).
6 Reinhart Koselleck, 'Einige Fragen an die Begriffsgeschichte von "Krise",' in *Über die Krise. Castelgandolfo Gespräche*, ed. Krzysztof Michalski (Stuttgart: Klett Cotta, 1986), 76 quoted from Stefan-Ludwig Hoffmann, *Der Riss in der Zeit. Kosellecks ungeschriebene Historik* (Berlin: Suhrkamp, 2023), 324.
7 Dipesh Chakrabarty, 'The Planet: An Emergent Humanist Category,' *Critical Inquiry* 46(1), 2019: 1–31; Dipesh Chakrabarty, *The Climate of History in a Planetary Age* (Chicago: Chicago University Press, 2021).
8 Achille Mbembe, *Politique de l'inimitié* (Paris: La Découverte, 2016).
9 For a discussion of the term teleology, see Henning Trüper, Dipesh Chakrabarty, and Sanjay Subrahmanyam (eds), *Historical Teleologies in the Modern World* (London: Bloomsbury, 2015).
10 Bo Stråth, *The Brandt Commission and the Multinationals. Planetary Perspectives* (London: Routledge, 2023).
11 Koselleck, *Kritik und Krise*.
12 Dipesh Chakrabarty, *Provincializing Europe. Postcolonial Thought and Historical Difference* (Princeton: Princeton University Press, 2000).
13 Bo Stråth, "Provincializing for a Planetary Perspective." *Práticas da História*, no. 11 (2020): 225–46.
14 Walter Benjamin, 'On Language as Such and on the Language of Man,' in *One-Way Street and Other Writings*, trans. Edmund Jephcott and Kingsway Shorter (London: NLB, 1979 [1916]), 107–23; Walter Benjamin, 'The Task of the Translator,' in *Illuminations*, trans. Harry Zohn, ed. with an Intro. by Hannah Arendt (London: Fontana, 1992). Both references quoted from Winnfried Menninghaus, *Walter Benjamins Theorie der Sprachmagie* (Frankfurt am Main: Suhrkamp, 1995).
15 For an exploration of the translations of the semantics of the social and the economic between European and Asian languages, see Hagen Schulz-Forberg (ed), *A Global Conceptual History of Asia* (London: Pickering & Chatto, 2014). See also for arguments about such translations Bo Stråth, 'Comparative Conceptual History and Global Translations: An Outline of a Research Agenda,' in *Diskurs, Politik, Identität/Discourse, Politics, Identity*, ed. R. de Cillia et al. (Tübingen: Stauffenburg Verlag, 2010).
16 The Arusha Declaration was made in Swahili. 'Azimio la Arusha la 1967,' in *Miongozo Miwili Kupaa na Kutunguliwa kwa Azimio la Arusha*, ed. Bashiru Ally, Saida Yahya-Othman and Issa G. Shivji (Dar es Salaam: Chuo Kikuu cha Dar es Salaam, 2013), 23–42. The English translation is: 'The Arusha Declaration,' transcribed by A. Madyibi. For the speech act approach, see Quentin Skinner, *Visions of Politics, vol. 1: Regarding Method* (Cambridge: Cambridge University Press, 2003), drawing on the language philosophy of John Langshaw Austin, see, for instance, *Sense and Sensibilia* (Oxford: Oxford University Press, 1962).
17 Margaret Canovan, 'Politics as Culture: Hannah Arendt and the Public Realm,' *History of Political Thought* 6(3), 1985: 617–42. Cf Bo Stråth, *The Brandt Commission and the Multinationals. Planetary Perspectives* (London: Routledge, 2023), 18.

18 For this bias, see Martti Koskenniemi, *The Gentle Civilizer of Nations. The Rise and Fall of International Law 1870-1960* (Cambridge: Cambridge University Press, 2001).
19 Bo Stråth, *The Brandt Commission*, Ch 4.

References

Arendt, Hannah. *The Human Condition*. Chicago: Chicago University Press, 1958.
Austin, John Langshaw. *Sense and Sensibilia*. Oxford: Oxford University Press, 1962.
"Azimio la Arusha la 1967." In *Miongozo Miwili Kupaa na Kutunguliwa kwa Azimio la Arusha*, edited by Ally Bashiru, Saida Yahya-Othman and Issa G. Shivji, 23–42. Dar es Salaam: Chuo Kikuu cha Dar es Salaam, 2013.
Benjamin, Walter. "On Language as Such and on the Language of Man." In *One-Way Street and Other Writings*, translated by Edmund Jephcott and Kingsway Shorter, 107–123. London: NLB, 1979.
———. "The Task of the Translator. An Introduction to the Translation of Baudelaire's *Tableaux parisiens*." In *Illuminations – Essays and Reflections*, translated by Harry Zohn, edited and with an introduction by Hannah Arendt, 69–82. London: Fontana, 1992.
Canovan, Margaret. "Politics as Culture: Hannah Arendt and the Public Realm." *History of Political Thought* 6, no. 3 (1985): 617–42.
Césaire, Aimé. *Discourse on Capitalism*. Transl. Joan Pinkham. New York: Monthly Review 1972. French original *Discours sur le capitalism* 1955.
Chakrabarty, Dipesh. *Provincializing Europe. Postcolonial Thought and Historical Difference*. Princeton: Princeton University Press, 2000.
———. *The Climate of History in a Planetary Age*. Chicago: Chicago University Press, 2021.
———. "The Planet: An Emergent Humanist Category." *Critical Inquiry* 46, no. 1 (2019): 1–31.
———. *One Planet, Many Worlds. The Climate Parallax*. Waltham: Mass: Brandeis University Press, 2023.
Hoffmann, Stefan-Ludwig. *Der Riss in der Zeit. Kosellecks ungeschriebene Historik*. Berlin: Suhrkamp, 2023.
Koselleck, Reinhart. "Einige Fragen an die Begriffsgeschichte von 'Krise'." In *Über die Krise. Castelgandolfo Gespräche 1985*, edited by Krzysztof Michalski. Stuttgart: Klett-Cotta, 1986, 64–77.
———. *Kritik und Krise. Eine Studie zur Pathogenese der bürgerlichen Welt*. Frankfurt am Main: Suhrkamp, 1973 [1959]. Engl. transl. *Critique and Crisis: Enlightenment and the Pathogenesis of Modern Society*. Oxford: Berg, 1988.
Koskenniemi, Martti. *The Gentle Civilizer of Nations. The Rise and Fall of International Law 1870-1960*. Cambridge: Cambridge University Press, 2001.
Latour, Bruno and Dipesh Chakrabarty. "Conflicts of Planetary Proportions." *Journal of Philosophy of History* 14, no. 3 (2020), 419–454.
Mbembe, Achille. *Politique de l'inimitié*. Paris: La Découverte, 2016.
Menninghaus, Winnifried. *Walter Benjamins Theorie der Sprachmagie*. Frankfurt am Main: Suhrkamp, 1995.
Müller, Retief. "Afrikaner Missionaries and the Slippery Slope of Praying for Rain." *Exchange* 46, no. 1 (2017): 29–45. https://doi.org/10.1163/1572543X-12341429.
Schulz-Forberg, Hagen, ed. *A Global Conceptual History of Asia*. London: Pickering & Chatto, 2014.
Skinner, Quentin. *Visions of Politics, vol. 1: Regarding Method*. Cambridge: Cambridge University Press, 2003.

Stråth, Bo. "Comparative Conceptual History and Global Translations: An Outline of a Research Agenda." In *Diskurs, Politik, Identität/Discourse, Politics, Identity*, edited by Rudolf de Cillia, Helmut Gruber, Michal Krzyzanowski and Florian Menz, 213–20. Tübingen: Stauffenburg Verlag, 2010.

———. "Provincializing for a Planetary Perspective." *Práticas da História*, no. 11 (2020): 225–40.

———. *The Brandt Commission and the Multinationals. Planetary Perspectives*. London: Routledge, 2023.

Trüper, Henning, Dipesh Chakrabarty and Sanjay Subrahmanyam, eds. *Historical Teleologies in the Modern World*. London: Bloomsbury, 2015.

2 *Ujamaa*

Evasive and elusive African socialism

Nyerere and the concept of ujamaa
Nyerere's speech act moment
Visions of community, freedom, and exploitation
Visions of social justice and sacrifices made for the nation
The village community: contradictions within a political program
Ujamaa and development: contradictions within a concept
Continuities of the colonial heritage
The new master
The world stage
Experiences of disappointment and the philosophers

Nyerere and the concept of ujamaa

The *ujamaa* story begins in January 1967 in Arusha, an administrative centre located in north-eastern Tanzania at the foot of Mount Meru, close to Kilimanjaro. The President of Tanzania, Julius Nyerere, held a meeting there with the central committee and executive of the TANU, which, from 1962, had been the only political party in the country, and impressed them with his *ujamaa* project. After two days of intense textual drafting, the participants agreed, and the executive made a declaration on the policy of self-reliance with a key role for the concept of *ujamaa*. It was a remarkable moment. The Arusha Declaration spread like wildfire over Tanzania, provoking enthusiasm and even euphoria after a speech a week later, when Nyerere, in Swahili, addressed a crowd of almost 100,000 people in the capital, Dar es Salaam. He declared that Tanzania was an *ujamaa* nation based on self-reliance spurring them on to build a new nation with their effort and sacrifice.

The Arusha Declaration raises questions about the ambiguities and contradictions that arose from what at first appeared to be an unambiguous concept describing a newly independent nation and prescribing its economic and political ascent. Much of the subsequent confusion emanates from an evasive translation of what has conventionally been paraphrased as African socialism, a particular non-European kind of socialism. But the concept of *ujamaa* escapes perfect translation. The questions one invariably confronts when attempting any such translation deal with the ambiguities and contradictions within the mind of the principal advocate of the concept, and within the political economy that it outlined. They touch on decolonization and independence and the continuities and discontinuities within them. They are about the tension between the aim of resisting and the outcome of reproducing colonial structures. They are about the search for a concept that will veil these continuities in discontinuities and create new confidence that the future will be different.

The years between 1967 and 1974 were the heyday of the Arusha Declaration; short but epochal. Thousands of articles and books have been written about it, as well as about *ujamaa*, and many, or most, of them have ended in a confirmation of what was clear by the early 1980s at the latest: Nyerere's program was a failure. The intention here is not to offer yet another condemnation. Rather, this discussion attempts to recover the history of *ujamaa*, seeing it as a means to define Tanzania's postcolonial sovereignty and as a key concept in the creation and consolidation of the new nation. The chapter articulates the tensions built into the concept and the efforts to come to terms with them. It illustrates discursive power and its opposition, in other words, a struggle about shaping decolonization in the maelstrom of neocolonial projects and the emerging neoliberalism. Discursive power is about discursive struggles.

Conceptual history describes a different past from the retrospective *Besserwisser* ('know-it-all') view. It confronts and problematizes teleologies; in this case, it helps to escape arguments about how *ujamaa's* eventual failure was programmed into the plan at the outset. Conceptual history is about writing history forwards, not backwards. It focuses on the temporality of key political concepts, that is, their capacity to translate past experiences into future expectations. The gap between the imaginaries of the past and those of the future is continuously revised. 'Tradition' is not the essentialized and stable opposite of modernity, but the continuously renegotiated imaginary of the past, which serves as a contrast against which the contours of the future emerge. The future is open and continuously rethought, as is reference to the past. Both future and past are open, changing with the present. *Ujamaa* is about a prophecy that had to be continuously revised and adjusted to changing conditions. In what was assumed to be decolonial, colonial pressures remained. In what was formally independent, dependencies endured. These things belonged to the changing circumstances, which altered but, in many respects, persisted.

Nyerere's *ujamaa* theory was one of the most prominent attempts to revalorize African culture in terms of an alignment with twentieth-century European social, economic, and political theory. At the same time, Nyerere shared with those thinkers who belonged to an emerging ethnophilosophical movement, the thesis that key African values were communal rather than individual, and he endeavoured to formulate a conceptual and practical reconciliation between all the various influences and interests that constituted the communal.[1]

This case study of Nyerere's project investigates the practices and semantics around *ujamaa* and adjacent, apparently uncomplicated concepts like decolonization, sovereignty, and self-reliance, exploring their capacity to cope with tensions between top-down and bottom-up politics, and with both internal and external pressures for economic efficiency, which *per se* is a contested concept that escapes easy definition. The case study demonstrates the continuities across seemingly clear ruptures described by terms like colonialism, decolonialism, and postcolonialism, and between the bipolar world of the Cold War and its globalized successor of a supposed One-World, based on a unifying, seamless neoliberal market. It furthermore demonstrates that Nyerere's imaginary and implementation of national self-reliance was neither naive, idealistic, realistic nor cynical, but rather possessed all these dimensions in various and changing proportions. The case study finally demonstrates how the language of *ujamaa* permeated and was permeated by imaginaries of work, family, land, and property.

Kambarage Nyerere (1922–1999), son of Nyerere Burito, chief of the Zanaki, took the name Julius at his Catholic baptism at the age of 21. Following his school education, he attended university at Makerere College, Uganda. Aged 27, he received a British government grant to study at Edinburgh University, where he obtained an MA in economics and history in 1952. During his three years in Edinburgh, Nyerere travelled in Fabian Society circles and became a member of the Fabian Colonial Bureau. The Fabian Society was reform-oriented, committed to a gradualist, evolutionary socialism through the reform of the existing political system under the slogan of 'more haste, less speed.' The emphasis was on municipal rather than centralized state control. The Fabians rejected Marx's value theory, revolutionary approach, and hostility towards the state. Several of these ideas were recognizable in the Arusha Declaration.

In 1954, Nyerere established TANU with the goal of achieving national sovereignty for Tanganyika. Within a year, it had become the leading political organization in the colony. During the campaign for independence, Nyerere demonstrated his oratorical skills. After the first elections in 1958/59, he entered the Colonial Legislative Council and, in 1960, became the chief minister in what was still a British mandate territory. In December 1961, Tanganyika became independent with Nyerere as Prime Minister. A month later, he declared TANU to be the only legal party in the country. In December 1962, Tanganyika became a republic with Nyerere as president. In 1964, the new island republic of Zanzibar, which emerged through violent revolution, was subsumed into Tanganyika, resulting in the creation of Tanzania. It was against this historical and political backdrop that the Arusha Declaration was made.

When, in the Arusha Declaration, Nyerere translated his experiences of the Fabian society and what he had read about social Catholicism and Chinese land-labourer communism to the situation in Tanzania, he used the term *ujamaa*, which in its translation from the original Swahili to English is referred to as 'African socialism,' but which does not connote socialism in any European sense of the term. *Ujamaa* plays on the notions of family – *jamaa* – and kin group, and the abstractions 'familyhood' and 'kinship.' The family community became the carrier of socialist ideas, although Nyerere recognized that there was a dimension of exploitation, especially along gender lines in the precolonial Tanzanian *jamaa*, and of general poverty, which he sought to resolve in his theorization of *ujamaa*.[2]

This was something very different from a one-to-one translation of socialism. Nyerere used the term *ujamaa* to mobilize rural village communities, where the imaginary of an extended family as the reference point fitted much better than in the urbanized and industrialized societies of Europe. In the latter, the terms 'society,' 'social,' and 'socialism' referred to larger collectives unified not by blood but by their role as contract-based wage labour separated from the means of production. Of course, this understanding of socialism is only true as it was used in the nineteenth-century socialist tradition, and in particular its Marxist variant. Certainly, by the 1960s these terms had acquired a far wider meaning and a much larger history.[3] However, the translation of *ujamaa* as 'socialism' is nevertheless a solecism. On the other hand, the fact that in Tanzania in the decade after the Arusha Declaration there was a parallel debate on African socialism in the English press in Tanzania and on *ujamaa* in the Swahili press demonstrates how difficult it is to find a proper translation. From the very beginning of the translation of the Arusha Declaration into English, *The Nationalist*, TANU's mouthpiece, wrote socialism for *ujamaa*, for instance, without any reflection or debate on how much of *ujamaa* the translation carried.

If there was a parallel to the European term, it was to the early socialists, Saint-Simon, Fourier, Owen, and others. In the 1820s and 1830s, they offered new insights on coming to terms with social injustice, before the Marxists and social democrats closed the discussion through their competing exegetics on what socialism really was and should be. These were the early socialists whom Marx, not without contempt, called utopian. There are theoretical connections between the ideal of the *ujamaa* village and Robert Owen's family-based model production sites, or Charles Fourier's phalanx community, for instance. One might here also think of Gandhi and his Phoenix settlement in South Africa. However, the capacity to communicate a message and to mobilize people was very different in the mass societies of the 1950s and 1960s than 50 or 140 years before, in Africa as well as in Europe.

The concept *ujamaa* is of Arabic origin, meaning 'collect, gather,' and indicates some kind of community or collection of people. From Arabic the term spread into Persian, meaning 'society.' In Swahili the term also developed from Arabic to *juma*, meaning 'Friday,' as in *salat al-jum'a* (Friday prayers), also giving it a meaning of '(religious) community' or 'assembly.'[4] Zanzibar and the mainland coast had a long Islamic tradition, and in the nineteenth century in the interior of Tanganyika, Arab and Swahili traders established trading posts on the shores of Lake Victoria and further inland.[5] In the Indian Ocean trading communities along the East African coast and the Persian Gulf, key words to do with commerce and politics sounded different in various languages, yet were still recognizable as the same word. Arabic served as a lingua franca. There was in the term *ujamaa* a commercial, cosmopolitan connotation of trade community and commercial family and kinship networks while still connoting both a village and a religious community. For Nyerere, however, *ujamaa* went beyond this. It was about the nation; it *was* the nation. Nyerere feared potential divisions between Tanzania's communities and therefore looked for a unifying term; *ujamaa* was that concept.

As the Introduction argued, *ntu*, the Swahili synonym of *ubuntu*, was at the core of the *ujamaa* narrative: *ntu ni utu* means 'to be a human being is to have humanity,' '*ntu ni watu,*' means 'to be a human being is to be among people.' The *ntu* connotation gives both a moral and a social dimension to the *ujamaa* narrative.[6] Beyond *utu*, *ujamaa*, and *ubuntu*, there is a more general semantic connection to African philosophy with its emphasis on humanity as a community absorbing the individual. Society is community rather than (individual) freedom. Community is freedom and vice versa. Both *uta/ujamaa* and *ubuntu* reflect African philosophy and African humanism in this respect.[7]

The question of to what extent *utu*, as the normative underpinning of *ujamaa*, is derived from religious belief is unsettled. The concern with religion in the transcendental sense is absent in the post-1990 *ubuntu* discourse even though the early missionaries tried to assert this connection, as we will see in the next chapter. However, religion is not only a transcendental issue but deals also with a secular moral for living together, and in this sense, there is a religious dimension in both the *ujamaa* and the *ubuntu* discourses, in the former case with a more Islamic connotation, in the latter, more Christian. *Ujamaa* and *ubuntu* share with other expressions of African humanism in other regions and histories a lack of interest in the transcendental question and the non-human world. Of course, this kind of demarcation from transcendental thought in African humanism shared much with European humanism in its Renaissance as well as early nineteenth-century version, with the difference that the focus in Africa was on the human community and in Europe on humans as individuals. Another distinction is that in the *ujamaa* and *ubuntu* discourses there is no natural philosophy as a counterpart to the emphasis on humanity and humanism as there is in European philosophy.[8]

One might see a connection between this and the fact that the ideology of historical materialism is difficult to discern in African humanist philosophy. As already stated, although Nyerere's *ujamaa* project was often translated as African socialism, it was very different from the European versions. Nyerere's solution to this problem was to introduce *ujamaa* as socialism with an African origin, congruent with the traditions of African societies. He certainly wanted *ujamaa* to connote the creation of a better society, but the distinction between the traditional society and the future *ujamaa* society was not as radical as the equivalent movement had been in Europe. The value basis was the same, but in Africa there was no need for a revolution to bring about socialism. The way to a better future was to return to African values. *Ujamaa* as African socialism connoted sharing and reciprocity. This connotation connected *ujamaa* to *utu,* but without the sense that the realization of a new utopia needs the apocalyptic overstretch of the old world, the one appearing in the European Christian and socialist teleologies.[9] The use of *ujamaa* was considered a natural evolution of traditional society rather than one to be achieved through a violent and radical attempt to break with the past. This evolutionary perspective existed in other parts of Africa, too, such as in Kwame Nkrumah's consciencism. *Ujamaa's* connection to traditional values is underpinned by several Swahili proverbs and sayings, such as *kidole kimoja hakivunji chawa* ('one finger doesn't squish a louse'), appealing to reciprocity and communality. These proverbs provide the ethical and moral dimension of traditional values to *ujamaa*.[10]

The nationalist movement in the 1950s had mobilized around another Swahili key concept of Arabic origin, *Uhuru* with a capital U. The best single-word English translation is 'freedom.' With the capital U, it came to mean independence. It became the rallying cry of TANU and always came first when paired with other nouns in the mobilizing slogans of the nationalist movement: *uhuru na umoja* ('freedom and unity'), *uhuru na kazi* ('freedom and work'), *uhuru na afya* ('freedom and health'), *uhuru na ujamaa*.[11].

Uhuru was historically embedded in the history of pawnship, i.e., humans used as pawns, slavery, and abolition. In the 1950s the term was also used in colonial propaganda that sought to dissociate it from radical interpretations by instead offering 'freedom from taxation.' The colonial authorities and those who struggled for decolonization thus struggled over the meaning of the term. The TANU cadres promoted the slogan *uhuru na kazi*, 'freedom and work.'[12] There was contention over giving meaning to the term from early on.

After the achievement of formal independence, the drive towards an independent national economy required a mobilizing concept other than the cry for freedom. *Ujamaa* filled this gap and became the key word in this operation, separated from the earlier *Uhuru* to indicate that one was finally free and that the remaining task was to establish a new state, but at the same time maintaining continuity with the period of the heroic struggle for independence under the slogan of *Uhuru na ujamaa*. *Uhuru* was the past, *ujamaa* the future. *Ujamaa* became a central imaginary signifier for representing the future of decolonization. Nyerere did not coin his key concept in a void.

During the first post-independence years, Nyerere realized that the newly won freedom was limited by dependence on the international economy and the lack of trained Tanzanians. He began to dampen expectations that independence would mean immediate prosperity and government control of the economy. Nyerere travelled widely throughout Tanzania to explain that independence was only the first step towards full liberation, which could only be achieved by self-reliance and hard work. He became ever more the *Mwalimu*, the prophetic moral teacher who knew what was right for his subjects. In fact, the term was applied to him. Nevertheless, by 1967, the leadership of Tanzania experienced a political crisis of legitimacy. Farm workers had benefitted very little from the economic growth that had taken place since independence. Widespread disillusion prevailed. The Arusha Declaration was intended to address this situation.[13]

Nyerere's speech act moment

The Arusha Declaration was hammered out by the TANU central committee and national executive committee which had gathered for a weekend meeting between the 26 and 29 January 1967. Its Youth League, which had a national gathering there too, also participated in the work. Mwalimu, as Nyerere was called, arrived in the city towards the end of a two-week-long tour of the country. Over a fortnight, he had seen the living conditions of the population and, through his speeches and various discussions, had measured the level of discontent and developed the idea of *ujamaa* and self-reliance with the aim of improving things. He had listened and responded, not least by warning the party functionaries about their own lifestyles which were far above that of the people, and distinct from the principles and ideals of the party. Reports from the tour demonstrated a growing concern in the population, and Nyerere's galvanizing speeches were going some way to address the unease, but the question in the air was how to bridge the gap between the people and its leaders that had emerged since independence and how to motivate the people to make the effort and sacrifice necessary to secure independence through economic development. Nyerere arrived in Arusha with a plan to make Tanzania an *ujamaa* nation based on self-reliance. During two days of intense debate, he overcame the scepticism of several cabinet ministers by outlining the meaning of *ujamaa* and laying out his vision of Tanzania as a self-reliant nation of village communities.

He also led the process of drafting the declaration. The closed meeting took place in the social welfare hall of the Kaloleni community in Arusha. (For the tenth-anniversary celebration in 1977, the building was converted into the Arusha Declaration Museum.) On Saturday 28th, the delegates sat up until midnight to finalize the text. Others participating in the drafting process included Benjamin Mpaka, later a spokesman for the President and one of his successors, but currently editor in chief of *The Nationalist*, the party's mouthpiece, and Nsa-Kaisi, one of the *The Nationalist*'s senior staff journalists. In his memoirs, Mpaka remembers how Nyerere talked about his journey and his impression of the living conditions of the people. He relayed how articulate Nyerere was in his argument for the concept of *ujamaa* as the instrument of self-reliance. It was Nsa-Kaisi who came up with the name 'Arusha Declaration' and used it in a report for the paper. Nyerere liked and adopted it.[14] It was adopted by the meeting in the early hours of Sunday morning, 29 January. Nyerere left for the final leg of his tour later that morning. On the way there, he stopped at Moshi in the Kilimanjaro region for a stone-laying ceremony for a new police training college where he received a tumultuous welcome from the thousands who'd gathered to greet him. Their enthusiasm had less to do with the recently adopted declaration, and more thanks to various newspapers including *The Nationalist* and its Kiswahili sister publication *Uhuru* who'd tried, throughout the tour, to stir up a sense of euphoria.

The Nationalist set the headline "Document Receives Unanimous Vote of Approval" over an article summarizing the declaration. Positive newspaper coverage on the Monday began a well-orchestrated campaign to educate the public and glean their support for the Declaration.

Work by the government to organize support among both TANU party members and the general population also swung into action, the campaign ensuring that the meaning of the Arusha Declaration, along with the key concepts of *ujamaa* and self-reliance became universally understood. On the following Sunday afternoon, 5 February, people came in great numbers to Mnazi Mmoja Park in Dar es Salaam, opposite the TANU headquarters on what today is the Lumumba Road. "Excitement reached almost fever pitch as men, children and women poured" into the park, *The Nationalist* wrote. A record crowd of almost a hundred thousand (according to the newspaper) listened to Mwalimu. The Declaration and the work of the party machine in the days after its announcement precipitated an overwhelming mass response not only in the capital but also in many other centres. As on the previous Sunday, thousands gathered in Moshi to march from the regional TANU office to the Uhuru Stadion and listen, in the presence of government ministers and TANU functionaries, to Nyerere's speech broadcast by radio. According to *The Standard*, this was one of the most important policy speeches since independence. *The Standard* was a major, privately-owned newspaper targeted for nationalization, and which merged with *The Nationalist* as soon as it became state-owned. Moshi was just one example. The press reported from all over the country about plenty of enthusiasm and rejoicing. The newspapers told about a flood of mass support.

Nyerere's two-hour 35-minute speech electrified the crowd who responded enthusiastically to his charisma. Waving the Arusha Declaration above his head, he inspired them, converting them to his message and spurring them to work for the nation. He called on them, as well as on the leadership, to tighten their belts as they embarked, together, on the immediate implementation of the Arusha Declaration. The speech, in Swahili, dealt with its two major components: socialism and self-reliance, *ujamaa* and *kujitegemea*. While there would continue to be a place for private enterprise, key branches of the industry needed to be 'secured for the nation.' Nationalization was the key to self-reliance, but it was nationalization with compensation, not confiscation, Nyerere reassured the crowd.

The speech developed three general principles with detailed policies: Education as a means to fulfil self-reliance, or *ujamaa* and *kujitegemea* (which, in the English press, was translated as socialism and rural development), as well as freedom and development. It outlined four pillars for the implementation of *ujamaa*: the people, land, equitable policies, and good governance. Obviously, one of its main purposes was to bridge the chasm between the people and the leadership. Implementation of the pillars dealt with the nationalization of private property, the Africanization of the civil service and the reorganization of small, scattered farm settlements into ujamaa villages for improved social services and labour mobilization. The backbone of the economy was to be collective agricultural practice.

The newspapers reported the crowd's enthusiasm in their Monday issues. "Blueprint for socialism. Mwalimu outlines path for future," *The Standard* declared over six columns on its front page. "The Road to Socialism," *The Nationalist* wrote. It is interesting to note how, without discussion or hesitation, they translated *ujamaa* as socialism.

The speech was a speech act as the term was defined in the Introduction. To say something is to do something. Speech provokes action, and prompt action followed the 5th of February performance in Dar es Salaam. On the following day, a Monday, the government announced the nationalization of the banks. Later in the week, eight big flour-mill companies and other food-processing enterprises became state-owned, as well as the national insurance corporation and eight major trading firms. It was announced that negotiations would begin with other industries about the government taking a controlling share – a process very like nationalization – with the promise of 'full and fair' compensation.

The Arusha Declaration was not "just a high-sounding manifesto" according to *The Standard*. It was a "working resolution to guide a working political organization," guaranteeing the absence of exploitation through all working citizens' control of the means of production. The speech led to immediate action. At the centre of the declaration were the rural village communities, and at the centre of the rejoicing masses were the urban workers. Thus, from the beginning, there were contradictions between the rhetoric and the action that followed, and many more in attempts to transcend them. The revolutionary mood consisted of a sense of profound change and great rejoicing, without the idea of violence and bloodshed.[15]

In a 1979 publication, the government gave an account of the *ujamaa* campaign to unify the nation, which followed immediately on from the Dar es Salaam speech:

> ... immediately after the Arusha Declaration, it was pronounced in February 1967 that the priority was to raise public awareness of the Declaration so that they can better understand its objectives for them to participate fully in the building of Socialism and Self-reliance. The arts were fully involved in providing the intended knowledge. Dance groups, choirs and music ensembles created and performed songs which explained the values of the Declaration. Drama, recitations, and poetry pieces were also created and enacted before public audiences or published in books. Murals and sculptures too were executed for this course. All these aspects were intended to increase national awareness of the Arusha Declaration.[16]

So, besides the press, Maelezo (the Tanzanian Information Service) and Radio Tanzania – Dar es Salaam, (RTD), and art from February 1967 onwards, were key instruments in the orchestration and mobilization of the nation. Murals, paintings, sculptures, and other art forms were used by teachers as aids. The implementation of *ujamaa* through education was key. The Prime Minister's Office, in collaboration with TANU and some parastatal institutions, involved artists in designing and producing informative materials through wrappers for packaging, for instance, to reach both the literate and the illiterate populations. Dissemination only through radio would have missed segments of the population. Paintings and murals in public spaces showing hard-working farmers in the fields and dirty work in the mining industry heralded collective action, hard work, and commitment to the nation. After 1975, this genre increasingly acquired the features of East European social realism, portraying idealised heroes rather than current conditions. One might call it *ujamaa* realism. Another common subject was Nyerere teaching Tanzanian youth about the road to *ujamaa* and *ujitegemea* (self-reliance). A key artist was Sam Ntiro, who, in 1974, created the socio-realist mural paintings on the foundation walls of the future Arusha Declaration Monument as we will see.

26 Ujamaa: *evasive and elusive African socialism*

Ujamaa: *evasive and elusive African socialism* 27

Figures 2.1 and *2.2* The press conveyed the Arusha message translating *ujamaa* with socialism. *The Nationalist* was run and operated by the ruling party TANU as its newspaper in English. (*Uhuru* was the party's newspaper in Kiswahili.) *The Standard* was privately owned and nationalized in the Arusha nationalization program. Under state ownership it merged with *The Nationalist* under the name of *Daily News* and became the government's mouthpiece and *Uhuru* that of the party.

Visions of community, freedom and exploitation

Uhuru during the colonial period was, among TANU nationalists, connected to the term *unyonyaji*, meaning 'freedom from exploitation.'[17] *Unyonyaji* and its verb form *kunyonya* convey a range of meanings from breastfeeding to bloodsucking. TANU nationalists used trans-ethnic African idioms that understood exploitation by strangers as *unyonyaji*, metaphorically sucking blood or other fluids from indigenous people or a parasitic mode of life, such as a tick that lives by sucking blood from animals. Translated into English, the meaning of *unyonyaji* as sucking gets a sexual connotation which it didn't have in the use of the term in the *ujamaa* discourse. There, the meaning of *unyonyaji* was unambiguously exploitation. This meaning is underpinned by the fact that *mnyonyaji*, an exploiter, alternatively is called a *kupe*, a Swahili word for a tick. There was no unambiguous, pre-existing meaning of the term, and it had to be shaped out of a variety of meanings in order to make it function as a term for exploitation, while also implying a need to exclude the bloodsuckers from the community. This is the way conceptual struggles operate with the goal of giving key concepts specific meaning and assigning this meaning a general dimension. The semantics of exploitation and exclusion in *unyonyaji* was successfully linked to the semantics of community and inclusion in the *ujamaa* vocabulary. James Brennan has demonstrated how this connection became instrumental in separating out the enemies of *ujamaa* from the new nation: idle city-dwellers, Indian house-owners in cities and traders and merchant families in commercial centres, for instance.[18] The link between freedom and non-exploitation formed the basis of the strong argument that there was no room for parasites in the emerging nation. This link furthermore became efficient at preventing public political dissent. Opponents of the new order were marginalized as parasites. Opportunities for public criticism narrowed as *unyonyaji* was linked to *Uhuru* and *ujamaa* by way of a negative contrast, freedom from and community against exploitation.[19]

Ujamaa was a term that circulated in various translations, semantic fields, and practices. In a pamphlet from 1962 titled *Ujamaa*, Nyerere proclaimed that there was no room for parasites in the new nation and, in the same year, the government effectively nationalized all land.[20] There was an appeal in the term that gave it both a positive meaning and – through the link to *unyonyaji* – enabled it to serve as a means of distinguishing between friend and enemy, inclusion and exclusion. *Ujamaa* was, despite its rural connotation, not a nostalgic, retrospective term but a mobilizing signal for breaking through and taking off, an argument for modernization. *Ujamaa* called for a return to African values where there had been no room for parasitism, values that had been destroyed by colonialism. It was, in this understanding, a concept for Africanization and the shaking-off of the European heritage, for building an African alternative based on self-reliance, self-determination and equality. It was a concept that laid out a fiction for political mobilization.[21] However, *ujamaa* also connoted the colonial past in its emphasis on the civilizing mission program of village conservation and land rehabilitation in tandem with moral betterment.

The rural connotation of *ujamaa* as village community was of a different kind from that employed when, in the 1880s, German sociologist Ferdinand Tönnies made the distinction between *Gemeinschaft* and *Gesellschaft*, 'community' and 'society,' where the former was a nostalgic and retrospective category about to disappear under the forces of industrialization and the latter laid out a process of relentless development towards specialization, division of labour and alienation. *Ujamaa* contained both of Tönnies' categories and possessed an optimistic view of the future.[22]

The Arusha Declaration galvanized and mobilized the whole country. Nyerere became a hero, while politicians and state bureaucrats were blamed for the economic situation. The nationalization of key sectors in commerce, industry and banking immediately after Arusha increased the popularity of *Mwalimu* Nyerere. He appealed for the reestablishment of traditional values at the same time as he contradictorily argued that practices on the land were backward, unscientific, inefficient and ecologically irresponsible. Only close supervision, training, and, if necessary, coercion by specialists in scientific culture could transform them into farmers, into a spearhead for a modern Tanzania. There was considerable continuity with the colonial civilizing mission in this message. Nyerere's eclectic combination of African tradition and European modernity meant that the fiction of tradition was very much constructed in the imaginary of modernity.[23] The appeal to traditional values and the simultaneous rejection of traditional practices made 'tradition' a target to both identify with and take off from.

The point of departure for Nyerere's vision of *ujamaa* was the equality of all humans, the conviction that all citizens had an equal right to participate in government at local, regional, and national levels, and rights to freedom of expression, of movement, of religious belief and of association. Freedom of association in a polity where only one party is allowed is, of course, not freedom of association in any conventional sense, and Nyerere tried to obscure this contradiction with the caveat that freedom of association was guaranteed 'within the context of the law.'[24] The

Figure 2.3 Teaching, education, training, and supervision were key components of the *ujamaa* approach, here illustrated by one of the mural paintings of the Arusha Declaration Monument. Photo Dominicus Makukula.

law's listing of these rights reflected the UN's catalogue of human rights, minus the right to establish political parties.

In his 1962 pamphlet *Ujamaa*, Nyerere argued that the concept refuted ideas of class conflict, and he doubted that a word for class existed in any African language. There was an obvious gap between his idealization of Africa's present and the reality of robust class language in the streets of Dar es Salaam.[25] The language of *ujamaa* bridged this gap by arguing that the urban problems were caused by *unyonyaji* (exploitation), and the government's solution was consequently to get rid of these enemies of society. Nyerere's imaginary was mainly agrarian, making the term urban *ujamaa* an oxymoron.[26]

The first part of the Arusha Declaration was not only about human rights and liberty but also about public rather than private ownership. The government was to exercise effective control over the principal means of production and pursue policies for collective ownership of the resources of Tanzania. On this point one might at first assume a reference to ownership by the village community, but here Nyerere suggested rather a role for the central government. He used words that came closer to Western-style understandings of socialism: "in order to ensure that the economy of the nation goes well, the government must have total authority/capacity/dominion/right of ownership/possession/power [*mamlaka*] over the important means of making the economy grow."[27] The state would coordinate the economic activities at the village level through its ownership of the land and means of production.

The declaration, in its first part, also emphasized the government's cooperation with other states in Africa in bringing about African unity. The task was, first, 'to work with all the political parties in Africa that are fighting for the freedom of the whole continent of Africa.'[28] Second, and more ambitiously, 'to see that the government joins with other nations/states/authorities in Africa in bringing about the unity of Africa.'[29] The term for unity was *umoja*, from *moja* ('one'), with the prefix *u-* shifting the meaning to the abstraction 'oneness.' This was a vague term that said little about the implications in terms of political organization. *Umoja* could obviously refer to both Western terms, 'federation' and 'confederation.'

Visions of social justice and sacrifices made for the nation

The second part of the Arusha Declaration outlined *ujamaa* as a policy of receiving a just return for one's labour, where no person exploits another, but everybody who can work gets a fair share.

> In a true *ujamaa* country a person does not exploit another person; instead, each person who can work should work, and every worker should receive fair income for the work s/he does and the incomes of different workers should not exceed each other excessively.[30]

This statement does not say anything about how much one should work or how much pay one should get. Not to exploit anybody does not, as a general principle, say anything about where exploitation begins. Likewise, the statement that incomes should not exceed each other excessively is very general and leaves scope for a certain difference depending on the kinds and outputs of work.

The third part of the Arusha Declaration dealt with the term self-reliance and the nature of development:

> We have chosen the wrong weapon for our struggle, because we chose money as our weapon. We are trying to overcome our economic weakness by using the weapons of the economically strong – weapons which in fact we do not possess. By our thoughts, words and actions it appears as if we have come to the conclusion that without money, we cannot bring about the revolution we are aiming at. It is as if we have said, 'money is the basis of development. Without money, there can be no development.'[31]

Nyerere in this context pits 'money payment' against 'self-reliance,' money as a capitalist instrument of market operations or as international development aid against self-reliance, *kujitegemea*. The *ji* is reflexive, and so turns *kutegemea* from 'reliance' to 'self-reliance.' In translation, the term lies somewhere between 'reliance upon' and 'dependence upon.' There is nothing of the European liberal imaginary of free-floating individuals relying on themselves without dependencies. The tension in the European enlightenment thought between freedom and solidarity, between the individual and that of the community, is dissolved. What *kind* of reliance or dependency is nevertheless an open question: the state, the family, workmates?

The model country that Nyerere envisaged was agricultural. The thrust of the declaration described improvements to, and modernization of, an agricultural economy rather than its transition to an industrial one. The pillar of this imagined economy was the local village community. A great part of Tanzania's land is fertile and receives sufficient rain for agriculture, and the country could produce food crops both for domestic consumption and export. The aim had to be to increase agricultural output. This was the only road to development of the country. Everybody wanted development but not everybody understood and accepted this basic requirement for development, the Arusha Declaration argued.

The biggest requirement was hard work, *juhudi*, the declaration stated.[32] The average paid worker worked 45 hours a week, excluding two or three weeks of holiday every year. For a country like Tanzania these were quite short working hours. In other countries, even those more developed than Tanzania, people worked longer hours. It was not normal for a young country to start with such a short working week. The normal thing would be to begin with long working hours and decrease them as the country became more and more prosperous. It would be appropriate to ask the farmers, especially men, how many hours a week and how many weeks a year they worked. Many did not even work for half as many hours as urban wage-earners did. At this point the Declaration introduced a gender perspective to emphasize its argument. The truth was that in the villages, women worked very hard, at times 12–14 hours a day, even on Sundays and public holidays, it stated. It contrasted the work of women to the idleness of rural men.[33]

Nyerere spoke in Dar es Salaam as the nation-builder unifying all social classes provided that they worked hard.[34] In light of the economic situation, his concern was for improved economic efficiency and output. Nyerere's language mobilized the workforce for national progress by means of the concept of *unyonyaji*, which was used to exclude those who did not work hard. His point was that exploitation in the name of the state was not like capitalist exploitation as conventionally understood, but rather a necessary sacrifice for the national community.

Although the economy was agricultural, it was not a subsistence economy but rather an economy of growth. Self-reliance meant improving living conditions and standards, not just their reproduction. There was little talk about the scale of the agricultural enterprises; rather, the focus was on cooperating family farms unified in larger units. The village was at the core of Nyerere's political vision, but not in the romantic sense Western admirers wanted to believe. His biographer, Issa Shivji, describes Nyerere's approach to the village community as pragmatic. Tanzania was a nation of village communities that had to be mobilized for greater economic efficiency through harder work, and on this basis, agriculture would remain the economic core for the foreseeable future. Nyerere talked about people working in the village, *vijijini*, or being unproductive in towns.[35]

The village community: contradictions within a political program

Arusha was the answer to the failure of the economic modernization approach recommended by the World Bank immediately after independence (1961–1967), i.e., a government-controlled, heavily capitalized state farms program. Its aim was the formation of model farmers who settled in a village, assisted by modern technology and a management cadre. A number of these farms had grown out of colonial enterprises, such as the Groundnut Scheme. In 1966 the government abandoned the program because of a shortage of qualified managerial staff, and because heavy expenditure on infrastructure, buildings, salaries, and machinery did not pay off. A concerted effort was undertaken to rethink Tanzania's approach to development in general and to rural development in particular. The Arusha Declaration in early 1967 determined the parameters of the new approach with an attempt to depart from local self-initiatives linked to state responsibility, which merged bottom-up with top-down developmental approaches, with *kujitegemea*, self-reliance, as its most critical point. Arusha argued for communal production (1967–1973), which after a few years gave way to the program of the 'development village' and the forced villagization of the early 1970s.[36]

Beyond the general pronouncements on the importance of working hard and intelligently, instead of the earlier reliance on investments and machinery, the Arusha Declaration avoided concrete suggestions. Nyerere's September 1967 policy paper *Ujamaa Vijijini* was more detailed, but the problem remained the link between speech and action. The performative moment that followed the Arusha Declaration one week later in Dar es Salaam on the 5th of February, 1967, soon became a void through a lack of concrete political and economic initiatives to implement self-reliance after the immediate nationalization programme. Self-reliance did not propel itself. In 'The Arusha Declaration Ten Years After,' Nyerere commented on this development:

In my report to the 1973 TANU Conference I was able to say that 2,028,164 people were living in villages. Two years later, in June, 1975, I reported to the next TANU Conference that approximately 9,100,000 people were living together in 7,684 villages. This is a tremendous achievement. It is an achievement of TANU and Government leaders in co-operation with the people of Tanzania. It means that something like 70 percent of our people moved their homes in the space of about three years! All these people now have a new opportunity to organise themselves for local democratic government, and to work with the Regional, District, and Central administrations to hasten the provision of basic educational, health, and the other public services, which are necessary for a life in dignity.[37]

What Nyerere outlined in 1977 as a history of success had in fact begun to come unstuck and provoke political radicalization rather soon after 1967. Until 1970 settlement in the villages was voluntary. Then the 'frontal approach' began. The two million village settlers in 1973 referred to in Nyerere's statement represented only 15 percent of the population. Between 1969 and 1972 the process of villagization was slow. This was the implication of the bottom-up vision. In November 1973 Nyerere removed the element of voluntarism and declared that by the end of 1976 the whole rural population should have moved into villages. There was no prior planning, and village representatives were not consulted. The increase to nine million in 1975, a figure that grew to 11 million in 1977, was achieved through mass deportation with military violence, where many first had to build their villages and live under very difficult conditions for months or even years. In the wake of compulsory village settlements agricultural exports broke down.

Against the backdrop of this gloomy development, the ten-year commemoration of the Arusha Declaration in 1977 became a forceful appeal in art to the people to retain the initial dynamics and commitment to the project in a time when it was running out of steam. The Arusha Declaration Monument, *Mnara wa Azimio la Arusha*, was erected by the party at the centre of a roundabout on the Makongoro Road in Arusha. It was an obelisk constructed on four legs representing the four pillars for the implementation of *ujamaa*. The mural paintings on the foundation walls of the pillars were made in an urging and mobilizing style heroizing work that one might call *ujamaa* realism, an African version of the social realism in Eastern Europe.[38]

The *modus operandi* of *ujamaa vijijini* shifted in the mid-1970s to top-down instead of bottom-up. Free choice shifted to coercion. In 'villagization,' the paradoxes, contradictions, and tensions in Nyerere's political program emerged. *Ujamaa vijijini* rapidly became a campaign to villagize rural Tanzania where the ends justified the means. After 1973 the '*ujamaa*' dimension of villagization declined and in the end disappeared. The official term employed after 1973 was 'planned' as opposed to *ujamaa* villages, probably to distinguish them both from the failed communal-production regime of the *ujamaa* villages, as well as from the unplanned settlements and homesteads in which Tanzanians had come to live.[39] The shift from a voluntarist, bottom-up approach to a top-down assertion of state authority resulted from large parts of the land-labourer class showing little interest in voluntary commitment to the villagization plan. When he began the campaign, Nyerere appealed to the power of local self-initiative. His authoritarian reaction to

34 Ujamaa: *evasive and elusive African socialism*

Figure 2.4 The Arusha Declaration Monument erected by the TANU, renamed to CCN, ten years after the 1967 meeting. Photo Dominicus Makukula.

the lack of local commitment could only be self-defeating, but this was the path he took. Nyerere rationalized and justified villagization to accelerate development and improve health, education, water supply and other social standards. The unsolved question in his attempts to implement the policy was the tension between top-down and bottom-up approaches. The colonial heritage made a shift from the former to the latter difficult. Nyerere's vision was about community construction from below, where the cultivation of the soil would produce a surplus for market sales. The village and its medium-sized farms were his alternative to the plantation economy, and agriculture, not industrialization, was his alternative road to modernity. In implementation, the villagization programs after independence became top-down centrist projects allowing more intense exploitation and extraction of surpluses generated in the agrarian sector, where the extraction of surplus never became a public good.

The thought in the Arusha Declaration was that the government's control of the economy, with its development plan as a key instrument, would lead to self-reliance. The experiences of the first development plan led to the conclusion that gifts and loans endangered independence and the road to self-reliance. Gifts distorted the domestic effort. The plan also emphasized the need to decrease the

Ujamaa: *evasive and elusive African socialism* 35

Figure 2.5 *Ujamaa* realism idealizing work as the key to the building of the nation. Mural paintings on the foundation wall of the Arusha Declaration Monument. Photo: Dominicus Makukula.

dependence on international financial capital. Instead of foreign finance, domestic agriculture was the road to development and self-reliance.[40] After the declaration in Arusha, the government proclaimed, as we saw, the nationalization of all banks and large plantations and industrial enterprises. The economy became state-controlled.

The Arusha Declaration was a call for revolution although not a call to arms. It went beyond an attitude of mind to concrete action with the nationalization of large plantations, banks, insurance providers and wholesale businesses, while also imposing 'leadership conditions' on top state and party leaders and civil servants, forbidding them from owning shares in private companies or rental properties. They could not have more than one income and were barred from using their public positions to accumulate private wealth. The revolution without violence was to be made from the top with the support of the masses in a mix of agricultural populism and Leninist elitism.[41] Nyerere's biographer Issa Shivji referred to the development as kulak *ujamaa*.[42] Better off farm labourers and local leaders used the villages to promote their own interests.

After the forced villagization, the agricultural workers began to politically distance themselves from Nyerere, who therefore began to lose his rural support base. Cooperatives, which had played a major role in the 1950s and 1960s, were abolished by decree in 1976 and state authorities obtained monopoly powers to buy crops, transferring surplus from the farmers to the state bureaucracy. As the economy declined, the state and the party became increasingly authoritarian. In 1978, Idi Amin attacked Tanzania to divert his country's attention from its domestic political problems. The war with Uganda was costly for Tanzania and further depressed the economy. Even if the successful defence eventually overthrew Idi Amin, the price was high. Commodities disappeared from shelves and traders and smugglers took over their distribution. Foreign exchange for importing raw materials and spare parts sank to a minimum. Corruption became endemic. The army flexed its muscles after its success against Idi Amin and a coup attempt in 1982 was very nearly successful. Negotiations with the IMF and the World Bank dragged on against the backdrop of a paradigm shift in the world economy which demonstrated how difficult it was to realize self-reliance and independence when one was stuck in a world of dependences but dependences that were about to change their shape, as we will see later in this chapter.

Ujamaa and development: contradictions within a concept

The image of Nyerere and Tanzania was tarnished by Operation Planned Villages. Nyerere revealed his contempt for the traditional rural mentality and his admiration of discipline and industrial organization, but nevertheless continued to be seen as leading his people through the desert to the Promised Land. The welfare and productivity argument for *ujamaa vijijini*, despite mass relocations, continued to make an impression not only in Scandinavian countries, the source of a large share of development aid, but also on Robert McNamara, president (until 1981) of the World Bank. After his term in office, the bank made a U-turn from provider of finances to imposer of austerity. Even though farmworker collectivization during the Cold War connoted Stalinism and the worst expressions of communism, there were international hopes for a better democratic future through the promises of the modernization narrative in Tanzania. Ideological identification with the modernization paradigm and its unshaken belief in progressive development was blinding.[43]

One of the most effective political strategies used by Nyerere was his public confession that he had made mistakes, such as in the 1980s when he admitted that he would not have done certain things if he were to start again. 'We were impatient and ignorant' in terms of local government and cooperatives, he said.[44] The belief in self-reliance through devoted work in rural villages did not resolve a constant tension between local achievements and externally extracted yields that enmeshed the economy in new dependencies. *Ujamaa* was for domestic use but had little power against external economic forces. The external world set the agenda and determined economic conditions. There was, in this respect, a continuity from the colonial to the postcolonial Cold War situation, and from there to the post-1990 world dominated by the austerity politics of the World Bank and the IMF. *Ujamaa* as nationalism was about local resource mobilization to guarantee national economic sovereignty in a world full of dependencies.

Nyerere belonged to the first generation of African nationalists. There was a tension between Tanzanian nationalism and Pan-Africanism in his view of Africa's future. His dream was to extend *ujamaa* to the whole continent, but he offered no precise account of how to realize this. Like so many tensions and contradictions in the political program he outlined for Tanzania, the tension could not be resolved. *Ujamaa* required borders for the community of self-reliance, but the Pan-African dream wanted to transcend or at least relativize inter-African borders. Nyerere and Ghana's Kwame Nkrumah were the continent's protagonists for the propagation of Pan-Africanism. However, they opposed each other in the search for a solution. Nyerere wanted to build the continent's unification bottom-up via regional integration projects whereas Nkrumah's approach was more top-down, preferably through one major decision at a summit. The colonial heritage continued to play a role in these considerations, not only the heritage of colonial borders but also of colonial law, which existed in great local variety in Africa (and Asia). Colonial law was the consequence of negotiation about the implementation and imposition of Western private law, with the guarantee of private ownership as its centrepiece, and the security of public order guaranteed by the power of the colonizers' weapons or by consent of the colonized, or both. Irrespective of their concrete shape in local cases, the power relationships were clear and the consent of the ruled was built on threats of coercion and violence by rulers. As British law crossed the seas it dropped much of its liberal ideological wrapping, coming to resemble a naked imposition of power more closely.[45] Independence did not come as a gift but had to be fought for and conquered. Struggles for independence were often a matter of clandestine, and revolutionary, activities. However, even if they were no longer clandestine, the struggles did not cease with formal independence. That was the insight that carried Nyerere to Arusha and beyond.

Ujamaa was, as we have seen, a mobilizing concept in these struggles, but the nature of the struggle set limits on the power of the concept. There was little scope for democratic pluralism with competing political parties, at least not of the kind that emerged slowly in Western nations through centuries-long struggles for parliamentarism. The struggle with or without violence in the colonies required elite management in what was referred to as bottom-up struggles for people's sovereignty. The backdrop of the imaginary of a sovereign people was that the people had representatives. The trouble was that they were not yet a people. This dilemma was obvious when it came to implementing the ideas of *ujamaa* and *kujitegemea*. Even if Tanzania's transition to independence was smoother and less violent than in many other African cases, the country shared the one-party approach of many other nations.

In elaborating his ideological commitments to *ujamaa* and 'one-party democracy,' Nyerere ruled out a multiparty system, arguing that the new state required the combined efforts of all in building a unified nation and in maximizing economic efficiency and social solidarity. He also argued that traditional African cultures favoured decisions by consensus. Multiparty systems were either artificial luxuries tending to turn politics into a game, or perversions of true democracy in that they solidified class divisions and inequalities rather than eliminated them. A one-party state could be even more democratic than one with two or more parties, Nyerere argued. Where there was one party and that party was identified with the nation, the foundations of democracy were firmer. At the same time Nyerere rejected the totalitarian organization of the communist state in which individuals were 'secondary to something called the state.' In 1962 he called for

> a strong political organization active in every village, which acts like a two-way all-weather road along which the purposes, plans, and problems of the Government can travel to the people at the same time as the ideas, desires and misunderstandings of the people can travel direct to the Government. This is the job of the new TANU.[46]

Continuities of the colonial heritage

Government policy in the 1960s was derived from a select elite whose members held top government and TANU positions rather than from the mass of the population because, as the prevailing rhetoric would have it, the population was still mostly uneducated and lethargic. The new government took on an appearance strikingly similar in structure and style to that of the authoritarian colonial regime. Nyerere clearly wanted a continuously self-governing society, but he also wanted to make certain that self-government served the right purpose, as he defined it. The new administrators were African rather than European and representatives of the same TANU that had widespread popular support during the struggle for independence. But to the locality and people whom they served, they were, in important respects, the same as the colonial administrators who had preceded them.[47]

Andreas Eckert has emphasized the continuities in Nyerere's agricultural politics with the colonial period. He portrays Mwalimu as a leader who paradigmatically personified the transformation of the African administrative elite in the colony into the ruling elite after independence with considerable continuity. This new elite was betwixt and between the local and the global, the old and the new. They occupied a position of intermediary ambivalence as cultural brokers mediating between different worlds. This position did not necessarily mean that the elite were torn between these worlds. In-between was as much a place to be at home as any other. The continuity was expressed as a specific understanding of authority, power, and culture, neither traditional nor modern, but a bricolage with a strong influence on postcolonial politics. This understanding was in the long run at odds with the promises of *ujamaa*.[48] Continuity shaped an alienated, demoralized, and uncooperative land-labouring community. British officials had sent numerous experts to Africa to help increase efficiency in the agricultural and industrial sectors and to restructure health and education politics, but development, for them, was something done to and for Africans, not with them, and Nyerere continued in this vein. The contradictions between formal, democratic, bottom-up participation of the people in local government institutions on the one hand and top-down control and manipulation of these institutions on the other emerged during the colonial regime but continued under Nyerere and eroded the principles of *ujamaa*.[49]

Nyerere's state was the agency of nation building and economic development, a unifier and organizer of society. The state suppressed the goal of independent initiatives of self-organization by the people as an instrument towards building up the self-reliance of the nation. In a contradictory way, Nyerere's *ujamaa* politics became politics for the people by the state from the top – authoritarian in nature and unwilling to devolve real power to local government or self-organization even while arguing for the importance of the decentralized village community. There was a considerable gap between rhetoric and practice. Nyerere read Marx and Lenin but detested the notion of class struggle, although this did not mean that he was a Gandhian pacifist either. Where all other means failed, he was prepared to support the armed struggles waged by the liberation movements in southern Africa. If Marx had been born in Sumbawanga, he would have come up with the Arusha Declaration instead of *Das Kapital*, Nyerere affirmed in an act of provincializing Western thought.[50]

In 1971, TANU adopted the *Mwongozo* document ('principles, guidelines, ruling order, regulative framework'). *Mwongozo* drew attention to the emerging contradiction between the state bureaucracy and the workers and became an ideological weapon that set off a wave of strikes, lockouts of managers and takeover of factories. In all, there were 31 actions that began in 1971. *Mwongozo* was a document from the left within the party and moved, in contrast to the Arusha Declaration, towards the language of class struggle, which was anathema to Nyerere. However, he kept silent. The strike wave continued until September 1971. In May 1974, he delivered his *Unapogoma, unamgomea nani?* speech, meaning: "When you strike, against whom are you striking?" His argument was that national enterprises were public property and were thus the workers' own property through the state. Strikes only hurt the workers themselves.[51]

The government was trapped between the requirements of the workers and the capacity of the economy, which, in turn, was a dependence of Tanzania's economy on international economic forces, i.e., global capitalism in the shape of the new phenomenon of multinational corporations, which began to defy and escape

40 Ujamaa: evasive and elusive African socialism

national political monitoring in the 1960s and, at the time, were the key target in the growing argument that decolonization meant neocolonialism.[52] Considering all the self-imposed restrictions and obstacles on the road towards the realization of Arusha, the decisive problem for the Tanzanian state as nation builder, with self-reliance as the target, was not the contradictions of the *ujamaa* approach but developments on the world stage. We will come back to this argument at the end of the chapter.

The new master

In Scandinavian countries, Tanzania was the 'shining star of Africa' and the Arusha Declaration became an icon. In the early 1980s the Scandinavian countries contributed a quarter of Tanzania's foreign aid. Nyerere's visits to Scandinavia were celebrated events that received a positive press across party lines into the 1980s. Norwegian historian Jarle Simensen has asked how this was possible. After all, Tanzania was a one-party state, with an oppressive security apparatus, hostile to private ownership and lacking an independent middle class. It was a socialist state, a farmer and workers' state in the vocabulary used to describe the GDR and stood in stark contrast to the Scandinavian development model built on pluralism, personal liberties, self-owned farms, independent trade unions and an entrepreneurial middle class. Simensen finds the answer in the hegemony of modernization theory, which guided aid thinking from the 1950s to the 1970s. Modernization was not necessarily linked to the issue of democracy but rather to a belief in development. There was a trade-off between development and democracy. Tanzania was seen as a transitional developmental state. While development might require authority for success, at the end of the road, democracy would emerge. The concept of 'social development' gained ground in the late 1960s when underdeveloped countries were reformulated to the politically more correct term 'developing countries,' emphasizing that they were on their way to becoming developed. Development theories became a core dimension of the broader modernization paradigm.

However, in the specific case of Tanzania, it was the Arusha Declaration that struck a deep chord in the Nordic mentality: egalitarianism, respect for practical work and physical labour, the role of farming culture in national life and the imaginary of family and village in what was seen as a modern(izing) social ideology. Nyerere's educational philosophy had a special appeal, as did his personal charisma. In his visits to Scandinavian countries, he emphasized the social democratic, Fabian dimensions of his program, which, according to a high-ranking civil servant in the Norwegian development administration, 'sounded like music to our ears.'[53] Political prisoners and mass deportations were repressed in a Freudian sense in this imaginary of a pure democrat. Nyerere's charismatic figure and eloquent argument for the compatibility of a strategy for aid transfers to Tanzania and the *ujamaa* strategy for self-reliance was tailor-made to suit political needs and beliefs in Scandinavian countries.[54]

In 1974 the Tanzanian finance minister stated that foreign aid now equalled 28 percent of the state budget; it had doubled in ten years. The main aim stated

Figure 2.6 Nyerere was a welcome guest among the Scandinavian social democrats. Here on a photo from a visit to Sweden in 1969 together with Prime Minister Olof Palme (left) and Tage Erlander, whom Palme just had succeeded on the post. The photo is symbolic with Nyerere between the new internationalist Swedish social democracy for a world beyond the Cold War with a Third World commitment, which emerged in the 1960s and to which Palme gave a face, and the older national welfare and Cold-War neutral approach that Erlander personified. The photo signals break-up. ABAB, Stockholm. Photo Hernried.

in the Arusha Declaration was self-reliance and independence from foreign aid. The finance minister referred to the 28 percent share as an insignificant portion 'absolutely necessary' for development, and Nyerere played down the goal of self-reliance and played up the argument of compensation for long-time colonial exploitation, the great price variation in commodity markets and the lack of international social insurance arrangements. During the subsequent decade the foreign aid share of the state budget rose to some 50 percent, accompanied by continuous economic decline. A financial crisis from 1983 to 1985 provoked the argument in the North that the economy could not support the state apparatus. From 1984 to 1985, the IMF and the World Bank, supported by the Scandinavian governments, required 'economic reform' as a condition for continued aid and loans. Conditionality replaced sovereignty as the leading principle in the development aid vocabulary.[55] Economic reform meant a tighter state budget and austerity politics. By 1981, the pressures from the World Bank and the IMF had already begun, and they increased around 1985. When the two Bretton Woods institutions required reforms to come to terms with the debt burdens and the financial pressures, they talked about "structural adjustment," by which they meant austerity politics for financial discipline. This was a decisive step away from development policies and towards the new radical global market regime. Rigidity and financial discipline replaced aid generosity, and the World Bank replaced the competing superpowers on the development stage (see this chapter's next session).

Under the slogan of *kujitegemea* (self-reliance), Nyerere had aimed for an economically independent Tanzania. While the educational aims of the Arusha program were attained, the economic approach failed, and ultimately led to a confrontation with the World Bank, and, in 1985, Nyerere's resignation as president. The conditions of foreign aid were no longer dictated by the modernization paradigm or Cold War competition between superpowers, but by a new, rapidly expanding market radical paradigm that in the 1990s would be called neoliberal globalization. In the new language, reform meant economic purification purged of social content. The World Bank turned away from Tanzania, as did its social democratic friends in the Nordic countries. In Africa, country after country succumbed to structural adjustment programs imposed by the World Bank and the withdrawal of crucial subsidies. Nyerere's rhetoric on the unfair world order and the need for the Third World to unify fell on deaf ears; Pan-Africanism was at its lowest point since decolonization.[56]

However, the basis of Nyerere's power during the first half of the 1980s eroded not only from outside, but also from within. The 1981 *Mwongozo* of the Chama Cha Mapinduzi, The Revolution State Party (the new name of Tanzania's ruling party after 1977 when TANU merged with Zanzibar's ruling party), was, according to Shivji "one of the most candid documents ever produced", and the work of the left in the party. It was written as a commemoration of the TANU *Mwongozo* in 1971. It openly declared that under the umbrella of the Arusha Declaration, a new class had emerged. *Mwongozo* talked about class struggle.

Nyerere could not prevent an eruption of the language of class struggle among the left within TANU and finally within the whole newly named party. At the same time, a right-leaning group was gaining ground within. The polarization between left and right grew. Edward Moringe Sokoine, Prime Minister from 1977 to 1980 and 1983 to 1984, stood for the last defence of Nyerere's socialism. He promised to 'uncover and sack all corrupt leaders.' He was killed in a car accident in April 1984 on his way back from parliament in Dodoma to Dar es Salaam. Few believed that it was really an accident.[57]

Ali Hassan Mwinyi (1985–1995) and Benjamin William Mkapa (1995–2005), Nyerere's presidential successors, led the transformation of Tanzania from a socialist state to a market economy under active guidance by the World Bank and the IMF. Mkapa had participated as a chief editor of *The Nationalist* in the drafting of the Arusha Declaration, as we saw. *Ujamaa* continued as a legitimizing term although it had lost its Arusha meaning and had become inscribed in a very different semantic field. After the introduction of the multiparty system in 1991, the political debate among elites and the middle classes occurred mainly within the framework of the neoliberal ideology of democracy, the rule of law, and human rights. At the same time, there was an upsurge of parochial racial, ethnic, religious, and narrow nationalist rhetoric. *Ujamaa* provided a consensual ideology, legitimizing political rule and promoting political stability, since it appealed to popular worldviews.[58] This consensual ideology was at odds with the development of a market-radical language imposed by the actors of the global financial markets, a market-radical language that emphasized competition for efficiency as opposed to consensus. More important than the term as such was the continued reference after 1985 to *Mwalimu* Nyerere as a legitimizing authority for Tanzania, even by politicians opposing his party.

The transformation of Tanzania from a socialist state to a market economy was much more than a matter of domestic politics. The shift was accompanied by the new radical market language of the World Bank, which set new parameters for developmental states. Market language provided the framework of Mkapa's campaign against corruption, with the promise to end it through applying the purifying mechanisms of market competition and privatization of state-owned property. The privatization process proved to be one of the strongest inducements to corruption, but that is another story.

The new World Bank-speak was an indication that the external structural diktats imposed by the Cold War, and the domestic attempts to respond to these diktats through more state power and a larger economic sacrifice of the population in the wake of failed centralized politics, persisted in new forms. The external diktats were different, but the experiences of the population went unchanged in many respects. The economy was not the open landscape that Nyerere and many others wanted in the 1960s, nor the instrument for self-reliance and self-realization ripe for harvest through general commitment to the newly won independence. Reforming the economy proved to be a struggle for scarce resources, which was not only a matter of a domestic interest clashing with a widening scope for corruption, but also of external power imposition, irrespective of whether it was the superpowers of the Cold War or the financial representatives of what was argued to be the one and undivided global world.

In the 1960s and 1970s Nyerere controlled the language of *ujamaa*, but in the 1980s the external market's radical language permeated domestic politics. The discourse of the receivers came to mirror that of the donors. *Ujamaa* certainly survived as a concept, although deprived of its original meaning, isolated and anecdotal, throwing some mythical light on *Mwalimu* Nyerere as a founding father of the nation. The dream of self-reliance in Arusha had little chance in a globalized world of transnational capital flows and global exploitation patterns.

Mwalimu Nyerere was like a chameleon playing on all three of Weber's dimensions of leadership: charismatic, traditional, and rational-bureaucratic. He performed as a teacher disappointed by the behaviour of ungrateful pupils, such as when he admonished striking bureaucrats, hidden in the shadow of the state administration, who in their air-conditioned offices became a target of popular dissatisfaction, which Nyerere did not hesitate to exploit when he referred to himself as one of the people rather than a member of the state apparatus. He talked about the unified village nation, but it was a unification based on both inclusion and exclusion. The urban population in general, and the Indian shopkeepers and merchants in particular, were outlawed as exploiting parasites and bloodsuckers in the language of *ujamaa*. Nyerere manoeuvred within the space between authority and anarchy and between top-down and bottom-up initiatives, in which he formed the nation through his arguments about honest work, including the strong moral message that work undermined capitalism and other external powers. The considerable number of political prisoners in Tanzania stood in stark contrast to Nyerere's demonstration of Fabian sympathies and his endorsement of human rights in the international arena, and his declining credibility among ordinary people at home was a contrast to his image abroad as a devoted leader and defender of democratic values.

The world stage

In the rich and overwhelming literature on the subject (some giving reference to colonial heritage, some not), Nyerere's *ujamaa* village project has mainly been seen as a failure due to domestic shortcomings, such as a lack of an efficient state administration, corruption, and the elite's plundering of the population. Others have condemned it as a utopian dream out of touch with reality and doomed to fail. It is astonishing how few references there are to events unfolding in the 1970s in the rest of the world.

At the time, much of the planet was preoccupied by Cold War geopolitics. The war was frozen in the North because of the balance of nuclear terror, but hot in the former colonies of Asia and Africa where the superpowers waged a variety of proxy wars in places where their geopolitical ambitions mixed with armed movements for independence.[59] Other than the Cold War, the world was also reeling from a paradigmatic shift taking place in the view of the economic-crisis-ridden North – a shift from Keynesian demand-orientated welfare economics (that were providing legitimacy for the Western side in the Cold War) to a supply-orientated, market-radical approach, which in the 1990s became the hegemonic tale of neo-liberal globalization. The shift that began in the 1970s fundamentally altered the preconditions of Nyerere's project.[60]

Concerning the competing masters of the Cold War, there were two events of lasting impact on Nyerere's politics which both occurred in 1971. Guinea, the rear base of Guinea-Bissau's struggle against Portuguese colonialism, was invaded by Portugal. The warning to Tanzania was unmistakable. Tanzania was itself the rear base of several liberation movements, including Frelimo of Mozambique. In the same year Idi Amin, supported by Britain, overthrew the government of Milton Obote in Uganda. Obote had supported Nyerere's opposition to British arms sales to South Africa. And Nimeiry declared Sudan a socialist country. A corridor of progressive states was emerging and Nyerere understood what this meant in terms of the risk of intervention by the former colonial powers, but he did not comply with calls to distance himself from this emerging formation. The Cold War was a bipolar competition between the two new masters of the world order, who tried to exploit the weaknesses of the new postcolonial states, but the old colonial masters still lurked as the Portuguese and British interventions demonstrated.

Immediately after Amin's coup, the executive committee of TANU adopted its militant document, *Mwongozo*, which analyzed the political security situation, and, against the backdrop of the military consequences and the growing role of the army, emphasized the need for the party to control the army and for the people to be armed. To control the army was to control the state. The document talked also about class struggle, as we saw. The state control of the army needed to have a clear dimension of the workers' control of the state.

The growing pressure for more economic efficiency provoked protests and attempts to defend what could be defended of the bottom-up vision once guiding the *ujamaa* concept. *Mwongozo* was about an order to regulate the conflict between bottom-up and top-down developmental initiatives at the same time as it gave a voice to the workers. After less than five years, Nyerere was losing control of the balance between bottom-up and top-down interpretations and the practical implementations of the principles of *ujamaa*. Political independence did not mean economic independence. The government was trapped between the requirements of the workers and the capacity of the economy. And the capacity of the economy was not determined by the vision of self-reliance but by international forces.

The Cold War, during which the former colonies became a battlefield, gave the decolonized states a certain scope for action by playing off the two superpowers against each other. However, this resulted in new dependencies on one of the superpowers, which undermined the protection of their independent status. Or they could try to stay outside the clash between East and West, a choice that had to be paid for with domestic discipline.[61] The Tanzanian dreams of economic strength, based on self-reliance through the bottom-up organization of village communities, faced the need for a strong state that could guarantee independence in a polarized world. A strong state required increased economic efficiency through imposing growing work discipline. The language that centred on the concept of economic efficiency emerged through the attempt to forge an alternative to political subjugation by the Cold War superpowers. The implication of this alternative was the growing exploitation of the population for the defence of independence. In other words, not very much had changed since the era of colonialism and imperialism.

When the economic world order shifted in the 1970s, the crisis that hit the West, especially the industrialized North, had deep implications for the struggle for decolonization and national independence in the colonies.[62] In 1971–1973, the entire post-war order, that had been created in 1944 in Bretton Woods around the dollar, the World Bank, and the International Monetary Fund, broke down. The collapse of the dollar provoked high inflation. Oil-producing poor countries in the South, which traded in dollars, responded by imposing an oil embargo, provoking prices to soar and sending shock waves through the North. This gave the South the idea that the same leverage could be similarly applied to other raw materials. In 1973 the leaders of the Third World, as the global South was by then called, demanded the establishment of a New International Economic Order, a NIEO, which would ensure a fairer distribution of power, resources, and wealth between the rich North and poor South. In 1974 and 1975, the General Assemblies of the United Nations became the arena for negotiating the South's claims. The initiative was with the South who, for a moment, knew what it felt like to be on the winning side of history, while the North lay sprawled in crisis. It was a *Kairos* moment; the perfect time to strike.

Transatlantic free trade maintained the public welfare economies in the Western part of the industrial North before the collapse in the 1970s. At the same time, the North held out the implied promise to the South that development aid would level up standards there. The narrative dictated that when resources moved from the North to the South, the South would be developed. And giving development aid was useful to the North in that it also bought political allies.

In the 1960s, increasing numbers of people argued that this arrangement was failing to lead to development in the South. On the contrary, development involved the South's continued dependence on the North. The idea that decolonization was in fact neocolonialism crystalized. Instead of the North helping the South, the South maintained the North's welfare economies through unfair trade terms. The neocolonial argument reinforced the feeling of Kairos in the South. And it was against this background, in 1973, that Nyerere, feeling that time was on his side, accelerated his village project for self-reliance.

The North hit back by rejecting the NIEO and imposing a new market-radical language. Inflation in the 1970s provoked growing interest rates by the central banks which, in turn, made loans more expensive, at a time (especially around 1980) when the South, exposed to financial pressures, needed to renegotiate terms with the World Bank and the IMF. The North rejected any requests to lessen the South's financial burdens, instead imposing austerity on the South and seeking to open its markets. In other words, the South, far from receiving the development aid it needed, was obliged to take a bigger responsibility for its own situation. In the new market-radical language of the North, Third World states were to be equal partners in a new, global, free-trade market, where global production chains moved cheap labour to where it was expensive and high-cost production to where it was cheap. The idea of equal partners provided the North with the argument to reject the claims for preferential treatment by their new 'partners.'

At the summit in Cancún in October 1981, the first joint meeting of leaders from both the North and the Third World, the American president Ronald Reagan signalled a radically new approach to debts, development aid, public welfare, unemployment, and the North/South gap. The British Prime Minister Margret Thatcher, who assisted Reagan in the new approach, met with Nyerere at the summit and asked how his negotiations with the IMF had gone. Nyerere answered that he had understood the austerity rationale that underlay the IMF package, but if he were to implement it there would be riots in the streets of Dar-es-Salam. IMF's request that Tanzania should devaluate its currency by 50 or 60 percent was impossible for a country like Tanzania with its pronounced primary production profile. Such a devaluation would prevent Tanzania from selling anything beyond raw materials and would radically increase its import costs, Nyerere told Thatcher. He didn't expect the IMF to write him a blank cheque, but it was impossible to accept such unrealistic conditions.[63]

The paradigmatic shift in world economics and world politics in the 1980s towards market radical globalization removed the preconditions for Arusha.

Nyerere's resignation as president in 1985 did not imply his disappearance as a Third World leader. Indeed, in Geneva in October 1987, he inaugurated the South Commission as its chair. It was an independent, expert-led inquiry into problems faced by poor countries and had been tasked to ask and look for answers to the question of why everything that had looked so promising in the 1960s had gone wrong, and to formulate a plan for the future.[64] It is interesting to compare the speech with his Dar es Salaam performance 20 years earlier. There is the same halo of charisma and the same programmatic approach, with the emphasis firmly placed on going one's own way, but the rhetorical ardour and passion of the 45-year-old president had been replaced by the contained frustration and repressed fury with a taste of bitterness of the 65-year-old ex-president. The audience of 100,000 Tanzanians in Dar es Salaam had in Geneva become a group of some 30 world leaders and experts of the South. One can't help but notice the difference between the inspiring message of hope in Dar es Salaam and the reflections on loss and frustration 20 years later. The opening address in Geneva outlined how the belief in growth and hope through development became a great disappointment.

Until the early 1970s, economic development took place almost everywhere in the Third World. The growth figures were impressive, and there was hope, Nyerere noted. "The prospect of relief, however slow, was strengthened because the whole world seemed eager to see it happen." Nyerere referred to the World Bank's International Development Association established in 1960 and to UNCTAD and the G77 group of Third World countries established in 1964 as well as to the NIEO campaign, 1973–1975. There had also been Willy Brandt's North-South Commission established in 1977 with a report in 1980 that caused great worldwide attention. Global poverty had been on the global economic agenda. But that time was now gone. The Cancún conference in 1981 organized to discuss the Brandt report became the beginning of the rapid erosion of the expectations it had provoked. It "signalled the death of any willingness on the part of the Wealthy States" to discuss the global poverty gap, Nyerere recalled in Geneva six years later. "There was a time when everyone seemed to accept the New International Economic Order… But no one is talking now in that logic."[65]

The South Commission was a follow-up commission to the Brandt report, but its argument stood in stark contrast to the Brandt report's planetary perspective and its message of one world. With the subtitle A World Divided, the South Commission's report in 1990 confronted the new liberal market idea attempting to unify the world in quite a different way than the Brandt Commission had proposed, but instead of taking over Brandt's one world vision, in clear contrast to the radical market liberal understanding of one world, the South report's strong argument was about Southern unification by means of "a self-reliant and people-centred development effort, through intensified South-South cooperation, and a restructuring of international economic relations."[66] There it was again, the idea of self-reliance, but now for the whole South in a new union against poverty and for development. It was a unification of the South against the North.

Experiences of disappointment and the philosophers

Influential African philosophers reflected on the politics of decolonization and the struggle for independence. They developed two approaches. There were those like Léopold Senghor who argued for an ethnophilosophy based on ideas of *négritude*, and those like Frantz Fanon and Paulin Hountondji who argued for a more universalist transformation of enlightenment thought, which had been developed and appropriated by the West, but which could also be used for resistance by the rest through an emphasis of its universal dimension and potential to strengthen criticism and support human rights, as opposed to viewing it as something specifically Western or exclusively an expression of colonial power.[67]

The generation of political activists who held out great hope for the future with concepts such as decolonization, *Uhuru* and *ujamaa* included Jomo Kenyatta, Kenneth Kaunda, Kwame Nkrumah and several others as well as Nyerere. They all found their efforts obstructed in the 1970s and 1980s. The clear-cut mobilizing slogan 'decolonization' shifted to the retrospective and reflexive term 'postcolonial,' which contained much more ambiguity and included within it no urgency for change. The new master, the World Bank, which replaced the superpowers of the Cold War, which had themselves replaced the colonial regime, represented a chain of continuities that contradicted the beliefs invested in the term 'decolonization.' Saïd's *Orientalism*, as well as Foucault's demonstration of the power of epistemic structures, underpinned prominent attempts to interpret the experiences of remaining continuities, whereas a term like 'decolonization' promised rupture. As ground-breaking, several decades later, was Chakrabarty's *Provincializing Europe*, which showed that the persistence of enlightenment thought and the imaginary of modernization and civilization was not only a one-way imposition of power, but also offered possibilities for resistance. There was a tension between Saïd and Foucault on the one side, and Chakrabarty on the other, about the potential for resistance. However, they shared the view that decolonization represented much less of a rupture and much more of a continuity and was much more complex than what the concept had promised in the 1950s and 1960s. They were crucial for the shifting conceptualization of the times from decolonial to postcolonial, with all its attendant ambiguity.[68]

Philosophers like Valentin Mudimbe, Achille Mbembe, and Patrice Nganang began in the 1990s to problematize the binarism between African ethnophilosophy and the universalists who believed in the potential of protest and resistance. They questioned the conceptualization of decolonization as rupture against the backdrop of the emerging disappointments after the initial euphoria of independence. In so doing, they exposed continuities as well as discontinuities across the old border between the colonizers and the colonized, and across the rupture of the present between a worse past and a better future.[69] The reflections by these three philosophers on such continuities and discontinuities and on concepts like decolonization and postcolonialism, freedom and independence, the universal and the particular, provide an excellent framework for the understanding of Julius Nyerere's dilemma and his struggle to come to terms with his key concept of *ujamaa*. *Ujamaa* was both socialism and not socialism, both Western and non-Western, and maybe in

Figure 2.7 Remembering the beginning of *ujamaa* with nostalgia in art. Mwalimu Nyerere teaching in the class. Education was a pillar in the *ujamaa* discourse. J W Masamja and Festo Kijo 1985. National Museum of Tanzania. Foto Eric Papian.

some sense also democracy (however one chooses to define this term) and autocracy. These philosophers also shed light on the ambiguities of the term *uhuru*, ambiguities that Nyerere was aware of. These ambiguities are not different from those within the Western concept of freedom.

Despite its failure, *ujamaa* persisted as a unifying term, much as Nyerere has remained the unifying father of the nation, even a cult figure.[70] The initial expectations of a future charged with potential for fundamental change and the widespread expectation of an imminent breakthrough and take-off have certainly disappeared. *Ujamaa* is no longer about giving certainty to an uncertain future but about giving stability to a present full of disappointments by reference to an idealized past. In this sense, the meaning of *ujamaa* has shifted to a semantics of nostalgia and now works therapeutically to overcome experiences of disappointment.

The abundant writings on *ujamaa* and what is seen as its failure, referred to at the beginning of this chapter, have conventionally analyzed the destiny of the concept from within, as an internal path-dependent development. This chapter gives much more attention to the role of external factors, in particular the changing faces of capitalism. As to internal factors, it is important to connect them to the colonial legacy which the newly independent Tanzania inherited, including the colonial state apparatus with its structures that remained resilient to change and a shortage of professional cadres. The *ujamaa* case supports the argument that the 1970s is a time worth investigating, not least because of the opportunity it offers to reflect on how and why things went in less-than-optimal directions as well as on lost possibilities and on options not taken.

Notes

1. Ivan Karp and D. A. Masolo, 'Introduction: African Philosophy as Cultural Inquiry,' in *African Philosophy as Cultural Inquiry*, ed. Ivan Karp and D. A. Masolo (Bloomington: Indiana University Press, 2000).
2. For the gender bias, see Priy Lal, 'Militants, Mothers, and the National Family: Ujamaa, Gender, and Rural Development in Postcolonial Tanzania,' *Journal of African History* 51(1), 2010: 1–20. About Chinese peasant communism in Chalmers A. Johnson, *Peasant Nationalism and Communist Power* (Stanford: Stanford University Press, 1962).
3. For the conceptual history of the term 'social' and derived concepts, see Raymond Williams, *Keywords: A Vocabulary of Culture and Society* (New York: Oxford University Press, rev. ed., 1985), 286–95 and William Sewell Jr, *Logics of History: Social Theory and Social Transformation* (Chicago: Chicago University Press, 2005), 321–8.
4. صلاة الجمع, *ṣalāt al-jumʿa* in close transcription; *salat al jum'a* in a more Anglicized version.
5. Gene Andrew Maguire, *Toward 'Uhuru' in Tanzania: The Politics of Participation* (Cambridge: Cambridge University Press, 1969), 4.
6. I am grateful to John Wakota for this point. See also Alena Rettová, 'Cognates of *ubuntu*: Humanity/Personhood in the Swahili Philosophy of Utu,' *Decolonial Subversions* 2020: 31–60 and David Leslie, '*Hekima* and *Busara* – Are They Different Concepts and How Do They Relate to *Utu*?' *Swahili Forum* 17, 2010: 24–33.
7. Luis Gordon, *An Introduction to African Philosophy* (Cambridge: Cambridge University Press, 2008), 186 quoted form Rettová, '*Cognates* of ubuntu', 32.
8. Rettová, '*Cognates* of ubuntu'.
9. Ibid., 47.
10. Ibid., 49.
11. Maguire, *Toward 'Uhuru' in Tanzania*, xxix, n.1.
12. James R. Brennan, 'Blood Enemies: Exploitation and Urban Citizenship in the Nationalist Political Thought of Tanzania, 1958–75,' *Journal of African History* 47(3), 2006: 393–4.
13. Andreas Eckert, 'Julius Nyerere, Tanzanian Elites, and the Project of African Socialism,' in *Trajectories of Decolonisation*, ed. J. Dülffer and M. Frey (London: Palgrave, 2011), 216–40.
14. Benjamin William Mkapa, *My Life, My Purpose. A Tanzanian President Remembers* (Dar es Salaam: Mkuki Nyota Publishers, 2019).
15. The account of the Arusha meeting and the week thereafter builds on *The Nationalist* and *The Standard* 30 January, 6, 8, and 11 February 1967. I am very grateful to John Dakota for assistance with source and illustration search.
16. Quotation from Dominicus Zimanimoto Makukula, *The Development of Visual Arts in Tanzania from 1961 to 2015: A Focus on the National Cultural Policy and Institutions' Influences*. PhD FU Berlin, Dept of History and Cultural Studies 2019: 226.
17. Brennan, 'Blood Enemies,' 393.
18. Brennan, 'Blood Enemies'; Andrew Coulson, *Tanzania: A Political Economy* (Oxford: Clarendon Press, 1982). For the role of the Tanzanian elites in Nyerere's project, see Eckert, 'Julius Nyerere.'

19 It is difficult to overstate how deeply the term *unyonyaji* came to permeate nationalist vocabularies. Brennan, 'Blood Enemies,' 394–6; Eckert, 'Julius Nyerere,' 227–8.
20 Julius Nyerere, 'Ujamaa – The Basis of African Socialism,' in *Ujamaa: Essays on Socialism*, ed. Julius Nyerere (Dar es Salaam: Oxford University Press, 1968). The original text appeared in April, 1962.
21 For a discussion of the role of fiction as 'a guiding principle' in nation building, see Nicholas Shumway, *The Invention of Argentina* (Berkeley: University of California Press, 1993).
22 Ferdinand Tönnies, *Gemeinschaft und Gesellschaft. Abhandlung des Communismus und des Socialismus als empirischer Culturformen* (Leipzig: Fues's Verlag, 1887).
23 Eckert, 'Julius Nyerere,' 230–33.
24 Nyerere, 'Ujamaa.'
25 For the Tanzanian class conflict, see Issa G. Shivji, *Class Struggles in Tanzania* (London: Heinemann, 1976).
26 Brennan, 'Blood Enemies,' 413.
27 *Kwamba ili kuhakikisha kuwa uchumi wa nchi unakwenda sawa Serikali lazima iwe na mamlaka kamili juu ya njia muhimu za kuukuza uchumi.* 'Azimio la Arusha la 1967.' This and other translations of longer sentences in this chapter are by Rhiannon Stephens.
28 *Kushirikiana na vyama vyote vya siasa katika Afrika vinavyopigania uhuru wa bara lote la Afrika.* 'Azimio la Arusha la 1967.'
29 *Kuona kwamba serikali inashirikiana na dola nyingine katika Afrika katika kuleta Umoja wa Afrika.* 'Azimio la Arusha la 1967.'
30 *Katika nchi ya Ujamaa kamili mtu hamnyonyi mtu, bali kila awezaye kufanya kazi hufanya kazi, na kila mfanyakazi hupata pato la haki kwa kazi aifanyayo na wala mapato ya wafanyakazi mbalimbali hayapitani mno.* 'Azimio la Arusha la 1967.'
31 'The Arusha Declaration.'
32 *Juhudi* means 'exertion'; *kufanya kazi kwa bidii zake zote*: 'to work with all one's effort.'
33 'The Arusha Declaration.'
34 Cf. Issa G. Shivji, 'Where is Uhuru?' in *Reflections on the Struggle for Democracy in Africa*, ed. G. R. Murunga (Oxford: Pambazuka Press, 2009).
35 Issa G. Shivji, 'The Village in Mwalimu Nyerere's Thought,' *Pambazuka News* 452, 13 October 2009.
36 Shivji, 'The Village.'
37 Ibid.
38 Makukula, *The Development of Visual Arts in Tanzania*.
39 James Scott, *Seeing like a State* (New Haven, CT: Yale University Press, 1998), 234.
40 Julius Nyerere, 'Ujamaa – The Basis of African Socialism,' in *Ujamaa: Essays on Socialism*, ed. Julius Nyerere (Dar es Salaam: Oxford University Press, 1968).
41 Issa G. Shivji, 'Nationalism and Pan-Africanism: Decisive Moments in Nyerere's Intellectual and Political Thought,' *Review of African Political Economy* 39(131), 2012: 103–16.
42 Issa Shivji, *The Silent Class Struggle* (Dar es Salama: Tanzania Publishing House, 1974).
43 Jarle Simensen, 'The Norwegian-Tanzanian Aid Relationships: A Historical Perspective,' in *Tanzania in Transition: From Nyerere to Mkapa*, ed. Kjell Havnevik and Aida C. Isinika (Dar es Salaam: Mkuki na Nyota Publishers in cooperation with the Nordic Africa Institute, Uppsala, 2010), 66–8.
44 Philip Mawhood, 'The Search for Participation in Tanzania,' in *Local Government in the Third World: The Experience of Decentralisation in Tropical Africa*, ed. Philip Mawhood (Pretoria: Africa Institute of South Africa, 1993), 101. Quote from Andreas Eckert, 'Useful Instruments of Participation? Local Government and Cooperatives in Tanzania, 1940s to 1970s,' *International Journal of African Historical Studies* 40(1), 2007: 97. Cf. Eckert, 'Julius Nyerere.'

45 See here Koskenniemi, *Gentle Civilizer*; Benton, *Law and Colonial Cultures*; Benton, *Search for Sovereignty*.
46 Maguire, *Toward 'Uhuru' in Tanzania*, 362–3. Quotation on p. 362.
47 Maguire, 363, who refers to H. Glickman, 'Dilemmas of Political Theory in an African Context: The Ideology of Julius Nyerere,' in *Boston University Papers on Africa: Transition in African Politics*, ed. J. Butler and A. A. Castagno (New York: Praeger, 1967), 195–223.
48 Eckert, 'Julius Nyerere,' 219. Eckert here also refers to F. Cooper, 'Conflict and Connection: Rethinking Colonial African History,' *American Historical Review* 99(5), 1994: 1516–45.
49 Eckert, 'Useful Instruments of Participation'; Brennan, 'Blood Enemies,' 394. See also, Mahmood Mamdani, *Citizen and Subject: Contemporary Africa and the Legacy of Late Colonialism* (Princeton: Princeton University Press, 1996); Frederick Cooper, 'Modernising Bureaucrats, Backward Africans, and the Development Concept,' in *International Development and the Social Sciences: Essays on the History and Politics of Knowledge*, ed. Frederick Cooper and Randall Packard (Berkeley: University of California Press, 1997), 64–92, and Frederick Cooper, *Africa Since 1940: The Past of the Present* (Cambridge: Cambridge University Press, 2002). For local government in Tanganyika/Tanzania, see Cranford R. Pratt and Issa G. Shivji, *The Critical Phase in Tanzania 1945–1968: Nyerere and the Emergence of a Socialist Strategy* (Cambridge: Cambridge University Press, 1976).
50 Shivji, 'The Village,' 108.
51 Shivji, 'Nationalism and Pan-Africanism,' 110.
52 Stråth, *The Brandt Commission*, Ch. 3.
53 Simensen, 'Norwegian–Tanzanian Aid Relationships.'
54 Alf Morten Jerve, 'The Tanzanian-Nordic Relationship at a Turning Point,' in *Re-Thinking the Arusha Declaration*, ed. J. Hartmann (Copenhagen: Centre for Development Research, 1991), 171–8.
55 Simensen, 'Norwegian–Tanzanian Aid Relationships,' 70.
56 Shivji, 'The Village,' 111.
57 Ibid.
58 Issa G. Shivji, *Problems of Land Tenure in Tanzania: A Review and Appraisal of the Report of the Presidential Commission of Inquiry into Land Matters, 1992* (The Hague: Institute of Social Studies, 1995), 149.
59 Odd Arne Westad, *The Global Cold War* (Cambridge: Cambridge University Press, 2005).
60 The brief outline here of the paradigmatic shift in the views on the world economy in the 1970s and 1980s is described and analyzed in more depth in Bo Stråth, *The Brandt Commission and the Multinationals. Planetary Perspectives* (London: Routledge, 2023).
61 For a hilarious example of the contention between the representatives of the two clashing Cold War ideologies in Tanzania, see Jamie Monson, *Africa's Freedom Railway: How a Chinese Development Project Changed Lives and Livelihoods in Tanzania* (Bloomington: Indiana University Press, 2009). The book describes how a Chinese team building the Freedom Railway from Dar es Salaam to the Copperbelt region of Zambia in the early 1970s clashed with an American team building a road from Dar es Salaam to Zambia with Western development money.
62 For the transformation of the world order in the 1970s, see Stråth, *The Brandt Commission*.
63 Stråth, *The Brandt Commission*, 283.
64 Inaugural Speech of the South Commission – UnitedRepublicofTanzania.com (accessed April 3, 2023).
65 The South Commission, *The Challenge to the South: The Report of the South Commission* (Oxford: Oxford University Press, 1990); Stråth, *The Brandt Commission*, 309–14.

66 The South Commission, *The Challenge to the South.*
67 Léopold Sédar Senghor, *Nation et voie africaine du socialisme* (Paris: Présence Africaine, 1961); Léopold Sédar Senghor, *Liberté 1: Négritude et humanism* (Paris: Éditions du Seuil, 1964); Fanon, *Damnés de la terre*; Paulin Hountondji, *Sur la 'philosophie africaine'* (Paris: Maspero, 1976).
68 Saïd, *Orientalism*; Michel Foucault, *Les mots et les choses: Une archéologie des sciences humaines* (Paris: Gallimard, 1966); Chakrabarty, *Provincializing Europe.*
69 Valentin Mudimbe, *The Invention of Africa: Gnosis, Philosophy, and the Order of Knowledge* (Bloomington: Indiana University Press, 1988); Valentin Mudimbe, *The Idea of Africa* (Bloomington: Indiana University Press, 1994); Achille Mbembe, *On the Postcolony* (Berkeley: University of California Press, 2001 [2000]). Patrice Nganang, *Manifeste d'une nouvelle litterature africaine: pour une écriture préemptive* (Paris: Éditions Homnisphères, 2007).
70 See, for instance, Chambi Chachage and Annar Cassam (eds), *Africa's Liberation: The Legacy of Nyerere* (Kampala: Fountain Publishers, 2010).

References

Benton, Lauren. *Law and Colonial Cultures: Legal Regimes in World History, 1400-1900.* Cambridge: Cambridge University Press, 2002.
―――. *A Search for Sovereignty: Law and Geography in European Empires, 1400-1900.* Cambridge: Cambridge University Press, 2010.
Brennan, James R. "Blood Enemies: Exploitation and Urban Citizenship in the Nationalist Political Thought of Tanzania, 1958–75." *Journal of African History* 47, no. 3 (2006): 393–4.
Chachage, Chambi and Annar Cassam, eds. *Africa's Liberation: The Legacy of Nyerere.* Kampala: Fountain Publishers, 2010.
Cooper, Frederick. *Africa Since 1940: The Past of the Present.* Cambridge: Cambridge University Press, 2002.
―――. "Conflict and Connection: Rethinking Colonial African History." *American Historical Review* 99, no 5 (1994): 1516–45.
―――. "Modernising Bureaucrats, Backward Africans, and the Development Concept." In *International Development and the Social Sciences: Essays on the History and Politics of Knowledge*, edited by Frederick Cooper and Randall Packard, 64–92. Berkeley: University of California Press, 1997.
Coulson, Andrew. *Tanzania: A Political Economy.* Oxford: Clarendon Press, 1982.
Eckert, Andreas. "Julius Nyerere, Tanzanian Elites, and the Project of African Socialism." In *Trajectories of Decolonisation*, edited by Jost Dülffer and Marc Frey, 216–40. London, Palgrave, 2011.
―――. "Useful Instruments of Participation? Local Government and Cooperatives in Tanzania, 1940s to 1970s." *International Journal of African Historical Studies* 40, no. 1 (2007): 97–118.
Fanon, Frantz. *Les damnés de la terre.* Paris: Éditions La Découverte & Syros, 2002.
Foucault, Michel. *Les mots et les choses: Une archéologie des sciences humaines.* Paris: Gallimard, 1966.
Glickman, Harvey. "Dilemmas of Political Theory in an African Context: The Ideology of Julius Nyerere." In *Boston University Papers on Africa: Transition in African Politics*, edited by Jeffrey Butler and A. A. Castagno, 185–223. New York: Praeger, 1967.
Gordon, Luis. *An Introduction to African Philosophy.* Cambridge: Cambridge University Press, 2008.

Hountondji, Paulin. *Sur la 'philosophie africaine.'* Paris : Maspero, 1976.
Jerve, Alf Morten. "The Tanzanian-Nordic Relationship at a Turning Point." In *Re-Thinking the Arusha Declaration*, edited by Jeannette Hartmann, 171–8. Copenhagen: Centre for Development Research, 1991.
Johnson, Chalmers A. *Peasant Nationalism and Communist Power*. Stanford: Stanford University Press, 1962.
Karp, Ivan and D. A. Masolo. 'Introduction: African Philosophy as Cultural Inquiry.' In *African Philosophy as Cultural Inquiry*, edited by Ivan Karp and D. A. Masolo, 1–20. Bloomington: Indiana University Press, 2000.
Koskenniemi, Martti. *The Gentle Civilizer of Nations. The Rise and Fall of International Law 1870-1960*. Cambridge: Cambridge University Press, 2001.
Lal, Priy. "Militants, Mothers, and the National Family: Ujamaa, Gender, and Rural Development in Postcolonial Tanzania." *Journal of African History* 51, no. 1 (2010): 1–20.
Leslie, David. "Hekima and Busara – Are They Different Concepts and How Do They Relate to Utu?" *Swahili Forum* 17 (2010): 24–33.
Maguire, Gene Andrew. *Toward 'Uhuru' in Tanzania: The Politics of Participation*. Cambridge: Cambridge University Press, 1969.
Makukula, Dominicus Zimanimoto. "The Development of Visual Arts in Tanzania from 1961 to 2015: A Focus on the National Cultural Policy and Institutions' Influences." PhD Dissertation. FU Berlin, Dept of History and Cultural Studies, 2019.
Mamdani, Mahmood. *Citizen and Subject: Contemporary Africa and the Legacy of Late Colonialism*. Princeton: Princeton University Press, 1996.
Mawhood, Philip. "The Search for Participation in Tanzania." In *Local Government in the Third World: The Experience of Decentralisation in Tropical Africa*, edited by Philip Mawhood, 75–105. Pretoria: Africa Institute of South Africa, 1993.
Mbembe, Achille. *On the Postcolony*. Berkeley: University of California Press, 2001.
Mkapa, Benjamin William. *My Life, My Purpose. A Tanzanian President Remembers*. Dar es Salaam: Mkuki Nyota Publishers, 2019.
Monson, Jamie. *Africa's Freedom Railway: How a Chinese Development Project Changed Lives and Livelihoods in Tanzania*. Bloomington: Indiana University Press, 2009.
Mudimbe, Valentin. *The Idea of Africa*. Bloomington: Indiana University Press, 1994.
———. *The Invention of Africa: Gnosis, Philosophy, and the Order of Knowledge*. Bloomington: Indiana University Press, 1988.
Nganang, Patrice. *Manifeste d'une nouvelle litterature africaine: pour une écriture préemptive*. Paris: Éditions Homnisphères, 2007.
Nyerere, Julius. "Inaugural Speech of the South Commission." Speech, Geneva, October 2, 1987. United Republic of Tanzania. https://unitedrepublicoftanzania.com/history-of-tanzania/mwalimu-julius-kambarage-nyerere/julius-kambarage-nyerere-speeches/inaugural-speech-of-the-south-commission-geneva-1987-inauguration-launch-meeting-summit/ (accessed April 3, 2023).
———. "Ujamaa – the basis of African socialism." In *Ujamaa: Essays on Socialism*, edited by Julius Nyerere, 1–12. Dar es Salaam: Oxford University Press, 1968.
Pratt, Cranford R. and Issa Shivji. *The Critical Phase in Tanzania 1945–1968: Nyerere and the Emergence of a Socialist Strategy*. Cambridge: Cambridge University Press, 1976.
Rettová, Alena. "Cognates of *ubuntu*: Humanity/personhood in the Swahili philosophy of *utu*." *Decolonial Subversions* (2020): 31–60.
Saïd, Edward. *Orientalism*. New York: Vintage Books, 1979.
Scott, James. *Seeing like a State*. New Haven, CT: Yale University Press, 1998.
Senghor, Léopold Sédar. *Liberté 1: Négritude et humanism*. Paris: Éditions du Seuil, 1964.

———. *Nation et voie africaine du socialisme*. Paris: Présence Africaine, 1961.
Sewell Jr., William. *Logics of History: Social Theory and Social Transformation*. Chicago: Chicago University Press, 2005.
Shivji, Issa G. *Class Struggles in Tanzania*. London: Heinemann, 1976.
———. "Nationalism and Pan-Africanism: Decisive Moments in Nyerere's Intellectual and Political Thought." *Review of African Political Economy* 39, no. 131 (2012): 103–116.
———. *Problems of Land Tenure in Tanzania: A Review and Appraisal of the Report of the Presidential Commission of Inquiry into Land Matters*, 1992. The Hague: Institute of Social Studies, 1995.
———. *Reflections on the Struggle for Democracy in Africa*, edited by G. R. Murunga. Oxford: Pambazuka Press, 2009.
———. *The Silent Class Struggle*. Dar es Salama: Tanzania Publishing House, 1974.
———. "The Village in Mwalimu Nyerere's Thought." *Pambazuka News*. October 13, 2009. https://www.pambazuka.org/pan-africanism/village-mwalimu-nyereres-thought (accessed April 4, 2023).
Shumway, Nicholas. *The Invention of Argentina*. Berkeley: University of California Press, 1993.
Simensen, Jarle. "The Norwegian-Tanzanian Aid Relationships: A Historical Perspective." In *Tanzania in Transition: From Nyerere to Mkapa*, edited by Kjell Havnevik and Aida C. Isinika, 66–8. Dar es Salaam: Mkuki na Nyota Publishers in cooperation with the Nordic Africa Institute, Uppsala, 2010.
The South Commission. *The Challenge to the South: The Report of the South Commission*. Oxford: Oxford University Press, 1990.
Stråth, Bo. *The Brandt Commission and the Multinationals. Planetary Perspectives*. London: Routledge, 2023.
Tönnies, Ferdinand. *Gemeinschaft und Gesellschaft. Abhandlung des Communismus und des Socialismus als empirischer Culturformen*. Leipzig: Fues's Verlag, 1887.
Westad, Odd Arne. *The Global Cold War*. Cambridge: Cambridge University Press, 2005.
Williams, Raymond. *Keywords: A Vocabulary of Culture and Society*. New York: Oxford University Press, 1985.

3 The translation of the unwritten
Ubuntu as religion, as law, and as politics

Ubuntu as a concept
The civilizing mission and the translation of values
The meaning of ubuntu in the minds of the missionaries
From a concept for sin to the language of emancipation and a critique of apartheid
Post-apartheid: ubuntu for reconciliation
The anti-neoliberal defiance and the new politics of social distribution
Reconciliation glossed over

Ubuntu as a concept

This chapter lays out a history of the concept of *ubuntu*. The concept became a mobilizing slogan in the 1990s, *the* key concept that inspired and spurred the South-African breakthrough towards new expectations after the collapse of the apartheid regime. The history of the concept began with Christian missionary colonists looking for a word in a local language (that had no alphabet) in order to disseminate their Manichean religious teachings about Good and Evil. As a post-apartheid concept, *ubuntu* became *the* key word for the reconciliation of what during apartheid had been oppressors and oppressed, Evil and Good.

Early history entails history as a written concept. It is difficult to have precise ideas about the use, frequency, and semantic embedding of *ubuntu* in spoken, preliterate African languages and dialects. *Ubuntu* is a word belonging to the Nguni language family (Zulu, Xhosa, Swati, Hlubi, Phuti, Ndebele) spoken in southern Africa. The equivalent Shona word spoken in today's Zimbabwe is *hunhu*, and in the Tswana language in today's Botswana and the South African Free State and Gauteng provinces it is *botho*.

Ubu- is a prefix forming abstract nouns, and *ntu* means 'person,' 'human being.' *Ubuntu* as the abstraction of *ntu* can thus be translated by inserting it into a semantic field of cognate terms such as 'humankind,' 'humanism,' and 'humanity.' At the time of the breakdown of the apartheid regime in the 1990s, a general and rather uncontroversial definition of *ubuntu* came from the Nguni proverb *umuntu ngumuntu ngabantu*, 'a human is a human through other humans,' a definition that emphasized the relational dimension to other people rather than individualism and made *ubuntu* connote community and abstractions like humanness and humanism. Nowadays, *ubuntu* is translated as 'human nature,' 'humanness,' 'virtue,' 'goodness,' or 'kindness,' and bears a positive connotation. *Ubuntu* thus connects nicely to *utu* in Kiswahili, giving a core meaning to the *ujamaa* concept, as we saw in the previous chapter.

Ubuntu has shifted meaning and political relevance several times since 1846 when it was first documented in writing. It has been a concept that has shuttled between theology and ideology, religion and politics. It has shifted between being an expression of Africanism and an expression of human universalism. Against the backdrop of decolonization, the term became a key concept in the search for African roots and authenticity and was used to evoke unadulterated forms of African social life before European conquest. In this respect, there is a parallel to *ujamaa* that spurred the Tanzanian decolonization and somewhat improperly has been translated as 'African socialism,' as we saw in the previous chapter.

The term was selected from local languages and given a written form by the Christian missionaries in the 1830s and 1840s. A century later, *ubuntu* began to connote precolonial and pre-Christian authenticity, genuineness and originality, something immaculate, unsullied. It expressed the idea of a specific African philosophy, ethics, or humanism, as distinct from Western forms of these categories. At the same time, the debate, in an ambiguous and partly contradictory way, also referred to *ubuntu* in more universal terms that went beyond Africa. At times *ubuntu* has been a weak and rather neutral concept without a particularly positive or negative flavour, although with a certain connotation of (African) universalism. At times it has been a strong political and/or religious concept with a negative or positive sense. Before the 1990s it was not part of public discourse.

An important point of reference in the conceptual history of *ubuntu* is Christian Gade, who in a pioneering work, scanned a great number of texts looking for the use of *ubuntu*. He found its first written mention in the Xhosa translation of the New Testament in 1846 and then listed the presence of the word in a number of publications up to the present, where his focus lies.[1] Gade has mapped frequency rather than substance in the use of the term '*ubuntu*.' He has not investigated the semantic field of the term in depth over its early use but rather has referred to it as a word generally meaning 'human quality.'[2] However, his mapping is a valuable point of departure for further explorations of the historical meaning and the significance of the term.

The civilizing mission and the translation of values

Before engaging with the concept of *ubuntu*, we shall explore the broader framework conditions of colonialism, the missionaries, and their translation work in nineteenth-century Southern Africa, particularly in the Cape Colony, or the Cape of Good Hope as it also was called. The work of spreading literacy and the Christian gospel in the world was closely connected to colonialism and the building of empires. There are many stereotypes and aphorisms about the role of the missionaries in their entanglement with the colonial enterprise, such as 'first the missionary, then the trader, then the gunboat,' 'first comes the missionary, then comes the resident, lastly comes the regiment,' or 'first they had the Bible and we had the Land; now we have the Bible and they have the Land.' They all contain a core of truth, but such relationships were more complex, and it would be wrong to simply dismiss the missionaries as mere instruments of the colonial powers.[3]

From the 1650s onwards, a Dutch trade and bunker station at today's Cape Town attracted a steadily increasing contingent of European settlers who penetrated ever deeper into Africa, with turbulent repercussions for indigenous hunter-gatherer and agricultural populations. In 1652, the Dutch East India Company occupied the Cape. Under Jan van Riebeeck, the Dutch adventurers and slave-dealers spread dread amongst and appropriated land from the indigenous inhabitants. Their initial idea was to grow vegetables to supply ships rounding the Cape, but their activities soon went much further, in step with the incremental appropriation of land. As we know, their arrival ended in a disaster for the indigenous peoples. Contact with the Europeans deteriorated further when the missionaries that followed began to preach about a God-given duty to civilize Africa, thereby lending moral righteousness to their cause. During the Napoleonic wars, the geopolitical importance of the trade and settler colony attracted the strategic interest of Britain. Aside from the brief recession to the Dutch Batavian Republic from 1803 to 1806, the British ruled the colony from 1795, finally and formally appropriating it from the Dutch in 1814. By extension, it became today's Western, Eastern, and Northern Cape provinces of South Africa. The missionaries, in the wake of the settlers, traders and military and civic state representatives, also crossed the Vaal River, moving into today's Free State, Gauteng, Mpumalanga, and Limpopo provinces of South Africa, and into areas of today's Botswana and Zimbabwe.

Keith Hancock's classic work on the expansion of empire (*Survey of British Commonwealth Affairs* (1937–1942)) conceptualized the development as a series of overlapping frontiers: the traders' frontier, the missionaries' frontier, and the officials' frontier with administrative and military power, where the missionaries assumed the role of moral guardians, seldom popular with officials and traders and often in conflict with white settlers. The missionary frontier clashed with the settlers' frontier and the idea of humane individuals working for the protection of the weak with the determination of a racial group to survive, to possess, and to dominate. Although the worlds of these groups probably were much less separate than Hancock suggested, there were many collisions and conflicts of interest between them.[4] Frontier life among clashing interests framed the work of the missionaries.

In the Cape, the frontier was conventionally imagined as an eastward movement where the clashes between the Xhosa and the colonists increased after 1770. In 2005 in a pioneering work, Nigel Penn explored another and earlier frontier moving north. On both frontiers the struggles were violent and ended in the subjugation of the native populations, but the earlier northward expansion from the beginning of the eighteenth century onwards was more open and expansive than that on the eastern frontier, which was more of a zero-sum game in which, in the end, there was only room for one power.[5]

The colonists, who destroyed the Khoikhoi, Khoisan, and Xhosa cultures, inserted themselves into a mythological framework that glorified this destruction, while the colonists represented civilization. They went beyond the borders of civilization, taming wildness and savagery. The near nakedness of the Khoikhoi along with their customs of 'eating loathsome food and speaking unfamiliar language' placed them at a lower developmental level, according to the invaders. When the settlers learnt that some of the indigenous inhabitants of the Cape did not keep livestock but lived as hunters and gatherers and were despised even by the Khoikhoi, they were convinced that such 'Bushmen' were on the outermost margins of human society.[6]

Richard Price investigated how the British established a culture of imperial rule in southern Africa in the first half of the nineteenth century, focusing on the interaction between the British and the Xhosa peoples on the eastern frontier. He explores how individual missionaries, military men, and frontier officials dealt with the Xhosa people and how they developed a knowledge system about them. His questions deal with how the British established and explained their dominion. In particular, he explores how the belief in the British empire as liberal was reconciled with 'the very dark things' that accompanied its construction.[7]

In the early nineteenth century the Eastern Province of the Cape Colony was a distant frontier of the empire that was difficult to get to and hardly a place in which to seek fame and recognition. It was a place where careers foundered and remained stuck. Grahamstown, the main settlement in the eastern Cape, was located 500 miles from Cape Town, accessible only over difficult roads or by a no less difficult sea voyage to Port Elizabeth. In 1820 the British sponsored an emigration program that sent 4,000 settlers to the eastern Cape to establish a new colony called Albany, imagined as a replica of British pastoral and aristocratic society. The year 1820 was filled with symbolic meaning as it commemorated the Pilgrim Fathers reaching New Plymouth in 1620. The dream ended abruptly once the settlers discovered that their equipment did not provide protection against the fierce weather, that their seeds did not take root, and that they were in the middle of a war zone between competing branches of the Xhosa people.[8]

Norman Etherington has emphasized that European missionaries accomplished little in the way of conversion. Christian missions certainly contained a dimension of cultural imperialism, but the agents of conversion were often local people. Native agents frequently supplemented the missionaries' exertions with translations and conversions. Christian beliefs were spread by ordinary people, whose numbers grew along with the colonial expansion. Unfortunately, the voices of these native agents, 'the evangelists' as they were called, are mainly absent in the piles of reports, letters, journal articles and other texts that fill the missionary archives. The voluntary mission and Bible societies that dispatched the missionaries faced constant pressure to raise money. Missionaries justified their lonely, underpaid existence by regularly writing reports aimed at pricking the consciences of contributors, celebrating conversions and explaining failures. For reasons of personal prestige, they also tended to play down the role of the evangelists and upgrade their own efforts. Descriptions of the hard-hearted, sinful, slothful heathen helped the European missionaries account for their slow progress in winning converts.[9]

Within this general framework the beginning of *ubuntu* was in the minds of the Christian English, Scottish, German and Dutch missionaries in the Cape of Good Hope. In the 1830s they were looking for words in Xhosa, Tswana, Zulu and other South African languages, words which did not have a written form, words which they could use in order to translate the language of a religion totally unknown to the indigenous Africans. Their difficult task was to find words for such things as a monotheistic God in language cultures that honoured the ancestors as holy, or for evil and sin, words representing a mode of thinking that did not exist in a directly equivalent form in the African imaginaries. The fact that the words the missionaries were looking for did not have a written equivalent meant that the missionaries were the agents that spread literacy through Africa.[10]

The missionaries, mainly Calvinist and Lutheran Protestants of various Evangelical and Pietist denominations, were well educated in the Bible and other Christian texts and had very clear conceptions of what they wanted to translate. They were Bible pundits who had learnt about the exegetics of the biblical texts in the framework of Bible and mission societies at classes and seminars they had attended before they left for Africa.

However, there is no one-to-one translation and the missionaries had to be tentative and approximate when they looked for relevant words in Xhosa, Tswana, Zulu, and other African languages. When translating, the missionaries had to struggle with the fact that there is always a gap between the meaning of a concept in one language and the meaning it is given in another language through translation. Translation is a tentative search for the approximate meaning in translations of what had precise meaning in the original language.

One must assume that the meaning of the Biblical words in English and German was very clear to the missionaries. At least some of them were also familiar with the Aramaic, Hebrew, and Greek original words. One might assume that they, despite this knowledge, thought and talked in English, German, and Dutch respectively, and that it was from there they were looking for relevant African words. Since the Dutch had been in the Cape Colony since the 1650s, they played a mediating role before the missionaries had learnt the native languages. Many Africans understood Dutch, which became a kind of *lingua franca* in the colony and gradually took on a creolized form later called Afrikaans.

To translate what was so clear to the missionaries was not an easy task, not least because they wanted to introduce a totally new order of thought about the world as it was known as well as about its unknown transcendence. In a time when there were not yet any dictionaries, only individually elaborated word lists that the missionaries exchanged among themselves, with a still very variable orthography in the translation of the spoken into a written language, they had to a considerable extent to rely on their intuition, and the precision in the translations was sometimes far from perfect. They had to operate with words and vocabularies developed for communication about things quite different from those that they had on their minds.

Robert Moffat, an English missionary in the region north of the Cape Colony border, noted how superficial many translations were when travellers picked up a word and believed that they had grasped its meaning. In a 600-page book about his life and experiences as a missionary in Africa, published in 1842, he gave several examples of getting lost in translation:

> I speak from experience when I say, that on some points travellers are very liable to be led astray. For instance, I once, while writing, heard a traveller ask his guide the name of the last halting place they had passed. The guide, not understanding, replied, 'Ua reng,' which the traveller, with all simplicity, was placing in his logbook; when, interrupting him, I said, 'What are you writing? That is not a name: he merely asks you what you say.' Accidents like the above frequently give rise to wrong names being applied to places; in other instances, 'mountains' was the reply, instead of the name of the mountain. And in reference to points of faith, or extent of knowledge, the traveller may be completely duped, as I was in the present journey.[11]

Moffat drew attention to the difficulty of spelling of placenames without a written language:

> Great allowance… ought to be made for the mistakes of early travellers in writing names and words, for nothing but long labour and observation can enable any one to catch distinctly the different sounds of what appears to proceed from a simple expression of the voice. Such individuals are often misled by interpreters who have but a very partial knowledge themselves, and what they have is merely picked up in a casual way, and without any regard to grammatical principles. … [I]t appears that each traveller and missionary adopted new names, which differed widely to those who had gone before, and who were the most correct. It is, however, difficult to explain why persons associating with the Bechuanas, should write Bootshuanas, Botchuanas and Moschuanas; Lattakoo for Lithako; Krooman for Kuruman; Mateebe and Matevi for Mothibi; and Bachapins and Machapis for Batlapis; and Bacharaquas for Batlaros, etc.[12]

Moffat gave other examples of misunderstandings in the translations and interpretations between the cultures. He told of how at an isolated village, deep in the wilds, he met an individual who appeared somewhat more intelligent than the rest; to him he put a number of questions to ascertain if there were any tradition in the country respecting the great flood, a theme encountered all over the world. Astonished to hear that the interviewee had at least some knowledge of the subject, Moffat began to suspect that he had got it from the Bible and asked for the source of his information. The answer was 'from the forefathers,' under assurance that he had never seen or heard of a missionary. Moffat was puzzled. The interviewee stayed for a few days in Moffat's travel group. At a village, Moffat asked a guide if he could take the group to a mission station in the neighbourhood. The guide declined but pointing to the narrator of the story of the flood he added: "*There* is a man that knows the road to Bethany, for I have seen him there."[13] The forefather who had told the story of the flood was a missionary.

The Anglican, Congregational, Presbyterian and Methodist missionaries from Britain, the Netherlands, the US, Germany, and somewhat later also Scandinavia, with an Evangelical or Pietist approach, shared a concern for personal conversion, Biblical authority and intense devotion in their dissemination of Christianity. They spread a culture of Evangelical and Pietist Protestantism based on the precepts of Calvin and Luther. The emerging religious profile in southern Africa was reminiscent of nineteenth-century North America. The difference was that the indigenous people whom the missionaries addressed in Africa were exterminated in America. The Evangelical and Pietist missionaries – the Catholics did not have the same presence as the Protestants in nineteenth-century South Africa – brought with them different ecclesiological and political experiences from European history, such as the Reformation and the French Revolution, state churches and free churches, experiences which they tried to translate into the new colonial environment.

Since no church had a clear majority among the white settlers, no established state church emerged in the Cape. Instead, a pluralist and voluntarist church organization emerged. Broadly speaking, the Anglo-Americans and the Dutch had a more activist Calvinist approach than the Lutheran missionaries from Germany and Scandinavia. More activists meant more conflicts with white settler societies and bitter internal political conflicts within the missionary community as to the issue of segregation or integration of black Africans in the parishes.

The debate on segregation or integration in the churches was lively. The Anglicans preferred black-white unity whereas the Dutch Reformed churches opted for separation. Richard Elphick and Rodney Davenport, in their collected volume on the political, social, and cultural history of Christianity in South Africa, provide many examples of divisions and plurality in what looked like a common front. They draw attention to this pluralism by demonstrating that, although most missionaries regarded Christianity and African religious views as mutually exclusive and even hostile, the interpretative practice and political-religious implementation of the two worldviews are best understood in terms of negotiation and accommodation.[14]

The mission enterprises went beyond national and colonial borders. The first missionaries in the Cape with a capacity to stay on, established their stations in the 1790s. Moravian brothers from Herrnhut in Saxony, Germany, built the Genadendal mission station in 1792. British and Dutch mission stations followed. The Prussian Missionary Society in Berlin, a Protestant, old Lutheran society within the German tradition of Pietism, founded by a group of laymen from the post-Napoleonic Prussian nobility in 1824, sent its first missionaries to South Africa ten years later.

At the end of the nineteenth century a survey counted 385 mission stations in South Africa run by 15 different mission societies. The mission stations were the hubs of the mission work. They were the centres formally supervised and financed by the Bible and mission societies in the motherlands but were often difficult to monitor from remote Europe. Therefore, they sometimes became local fiefdoms. The stations were often located in areas with settlers, and this often led to conflicts between the settlers and the missionaries about the exploitation of labour, which the teachings of the missionaries condemned.[15] Of course, it alaso happened that they had no objections to such cases.

The missionaries who worked from these platforms were, as Elphick has emphasized, less interested in disputes about denominational theology in the wake of their different confessional approaches. Their shared preoccupation was the issue of sin and the desire for personal salvation. The Protestant missionaries were remarkably united in their crusade for the conversion of the world. Their sometimes-bitter quarrels dealt rather with church organization within their societies than theological differences with other societies.[16]

A personal experience of salvation was considered essential to a candidate's 'calling' to become a missionary. They were all males, often married to women who had themselves undergone a personal conversion, and set out to awaken the 'heathen' through the transformative event they had experienced themselves. Some of them fled the growing religious scepticism in emerging industrial societies, hoping to build pastoral Christian communities based on an idealized European past.[17]

The missionaries came, to a large extent, from lower social classes: butchers, tailors, cobblers, cutlers, town clerks, carpenters, shoemakers, weavers, gardeners, farmers, and soldiers, but there were also impecunious businessmen and sons of teachers and small factory owners. Few of them came from the demoralized poor. They had at least 'rudimentary educations, practical skills, and an abundant confidence that the world was malleable' and offered 'abounding opportunities for those who trusted God and worked hard.'[18] Some churches possessed provocateurs of high social or scholarly status, such as John William Colenso, the disputatious Anglican bishop of Natal from 1853 to 1883, scholarly critic of the Old Testament, defender of African polygamy and champion of the Zulu royal house.[19]

The mission stations enabled these men of often humble origin to exercise their own abilities and offered them a new material security, comfort, and prestige. They were eager to maintain their power over people and events. In Africa they attained a professional status equivalent to that of the clergy in Europe. Their loadstar was the nineteenth-century conception of the Protestant clergy. The ideals of equality among Christians receded slowly to the background of their minds, and these once-radical egalitarians became benevolent paternalists.[20]

The missionaries were familiar with the religious discourses. However, they were more than that. They were writers and translators. Some were not interested in much more than the work of conversion, but many had a broader interest in the culture and the customs of their actual and potential converts. Some were or became philologists, with an interest in the native languages, and anthropologists curious to learn more about the custom, culture, and social life of the native ethnic groups. Others paid attention to geology, geography, fauna and flora, and some were interested in all of this. However, they were practical men as much as intellectuals. They had to be farmers, house builders, joiners, and blacksmiths as much as intellectuals and teachers.

The missionaries wanted to disseminate a gospel that was clear to them but, in many respects to the listeners, was quite new and difficult to understand and digest. This dissemination required negotiation and adjustment to the lives and worldviews of the indigenous people, which, in turn, required knowledge about these lives and worldviews. This process was not simply the imposition of a message. Rather, the process impacted on the message itself in what might be seen as a market for souls.

Utilitarians lobbied for English as the language of educational instruction in the colonies of Britain, but the missionaries often found it more productive to translate the sacred texts into indigenous languages for their converts, so that the local evangelists could communicate the gospel in the familiar dialects of their fellow countrymen. Making Bibles in new languages required the compilation of vocabularies and translations on a truly heroic scale, as Norman Etherington has observed. These translations were not only a matter of disseminating a new religion, however. Written language was equally important to the emergence of new identities among colonized peoples. In religious terms the newly won experiences contained surprises and contradictions such as, when reading the Old Testament in their own language, they found that King Solomon had numerous wives and concubines, while missionaries insisted on monogamy. Christianity took on a local character where new heresies opposed mission orthodoxies, and indigenous prophets denounced the oppression of settlers and colonial authorities.[21] Robert Moffat, in his field report in 1842, gave numerous examples of the problem of transcultural translation of religious thought.

The worldview and the religious beliefs that the missionaries wanted to change dealt with the search for protection among the shades, the ancestral spirits, often associated with certain spaces in the homestead or the cattle enclosure: a hut's doorway, the hearth or the space farthest away from the door. Ingie Hovland has studied the Zulus' various ways of communicating with the shades, such as leaving food near the hearth or being attentive to certain signs or dreams. The Zulu people also consulted diviners, *inyanga* or *isangoma*, who were in closer contact with the shades. Most of them were women. They worked as healers and interpreters of the messages of the shades. However, the most powerful diviners, *isanusi*, were as a rule men with authority to reveal witches and evil doers among the diviners.[22]

Retief Müller has in the same vein studied the rain and water rituals in precolonial southern Africa and the religious importance of these rites.[23] Moffat provided examples of the practices of the rainmakers and how they saw the missionaries as competitors in the area of prediction and prophecy, but also as equals at a higher social level than the ordinary people. They lived dangerously if they could not bring about rain or blame somebody else for droughts, however. It is a remarkable fact, Moffat noted, that a rainmaker seldom dies a natural death.[24]

Against these belief orders the missionaries presented their narrative, the Christian history of salvation, through their Evangelical Calvinist and Lutheran lenses, a history that began with God's creation of the world and continued with the sin of Adam and Eve and the flood. Original sin had contaminated all humans ever since. However, at the same time, the human was also the image of God in their narrative. Humans were thus both apostasy and divine copy. There was a tension in the Manichean message that the missionaries disseminated. This dichotomy was not always easy to translate. The dichotomy was of particular relevance when the missionaries used the concept of *ubuntu* in order to translate the human, as we shall see.

From this confusing conceptual framework, the narrative of Jesus, his life and deeds, his crucifixion, death and resurrection, took shape. The task was to translate a worldview, and this task required a language. A missionary who tried to win over a Zulu group of people called the serpent in the garden of Eden by the same name as the rapid lizard in the Zulu creation narrative: *intulu*. The serpent was equal to the devil. There was no other ready name for the devil, since the Zulus did not have an evil divinity, or a Manichean worldview of good and evil.[25]

The missionaries also needed a name for God in the native languages. There was in these African societies a lack of a distinctively superior divinity who was lord over all, omnipotent, active and personal like the Christian God. Colenso, Anglican bishop in Natal, reported in the 1850s that European missionaries translating into Zulu initially used several terms for God, such as *uThixo* from an imported san term, *uYehova* and *uDio*, *umPhezulu,* a Zulu term for being in the sky, *uNkulunkulu*, 'the Great-Great-One,' a Zulu term referring to the first ancestor, a senior shade, or someone who is very old. Colenso concluded that the Zulus had two names for a supreme being, although they did not 'know' it: *uNkulunkulu* and *uMvelinqangi*. He used the former term in his translations. Other missionaries argued that this translation did not quite match the Christian understanding and a debate emerged over Colenso's choice.[26]

Using the Tswana word for 'ancestor,' *modimo*, as a case, Paul Landau has shown how tentative and approximative the search was for native expressions and concepts for something that did not exist in the native minds. *Modimo* became the word for the Christian God. However, *modimo* had multiple meanings. The word also had a bearing on 'a missionary,' 'power,' 'past kings,' 'the station of one's ethnonym,' and 'a living king whose rule united a nation.' The ambiguity in this and other key words used by the missionaries sometimes gave the words two meanings, one meaning referring to the intended *replacement* of 'heathen beliefs,' and the other meaning referring to exactly those 'heathen' practices that the missionaries wanted to replace.[27]

Employing the word 'ancestor' for God, and thereby situating God at the origin of a long relational chain that lost personal contours after some generations, was not as uncomplicated as it might have seemed for the translating missionaries. The indigenous idea of *modimo* also signified, beyond this meaning, 'unknown force below ground.' Hence a Khoikhoi-speaking interpreter equated *modimo* with the Dutch word for the Devil. Only slowly did *modimo* take on the new meaning of God. Robert Moffat's translation of the gospels into Tswana in the 1820s, the beginning of his work on translating the New Testament, was crucial for this development. Tswana people began to read their own ancestral histories as versions of the Bible's stories of ancestral rule in Exodus and Acts. The relationship between *Modimo* and historical kings ceased to be denotative and became metaphorical. *Modimo* was 'the greatest king.' Missionaries and new Tswana Christians agreed that there would be no plural for *Modimo*. Ancestors (*badimo*) became the demons in plural which originally had no plural form. The precolonial Tswana *modimo* for ancestor became the imperfect version of *Modimo*, a remote and half-known God. The *badimo* had to descend to hell so *Modimo* could rise to heaven.[28]

The missionary preaching on issues like death, resurrection and life after death for Christ's followers was experienced as particularly funny, nonsensical, or disturbing.[29] Moffat found that the term *boleo* for sin did not convey the same meaning as it does in the Christian doctrine. The term connoted 'a weapon or anything else which they thought was not made as they wished.' Instead of asking whether *boleo* was the proper word to translate a thought which was unknown in the Tswana language, from his Eurocentric perspective Moffat noted that the locals called an imperfect knife or arrow a sinful knife or arrow. It was only to the missionaries that the knife was sinful. To the locals, *boleo* just meant that it was deficient. The Christian sense of sin arising from human responsibility had no conceptual equivalent in Tswana. The indigenous people did not even 'seem to think that the conduct of those who tyrannized them was wicked, but merely that it had fallen to their lot to be so treated, or was a thing that happened, like a lion killing a man.' When Moffat directed their thought to 'a great Being in the heavens,' some looked up 'with a vacant stare,' expecting something to appear.[30] Moffat talked with chiefs and ordinary people about divine things with little success. He referred to a discussion with a chief:

> Sometimes, when I have been trying to arrest his attention by repeating something striking in the works of God, or in the life of the Saviour, he would interrupt by asking a question as distant as the antipodes from the subject to which I hoped he was listening.[31]

Against the backdrop of such examples, it seems clear that the meaning the missionaries wanted to convey with a specific term might have been clear to them but often provoked confusion rather than clarity in the target group.

Lamin Sanneh has argued that when the Christian message was translated from the missionaries' frame of reference to that of the indigenous population, the native vocabulary had the final say as to the adoption of the message. The locals had the power of interpretation. The Western assumptions underpinning the missionaries' terminology had to yield to local presuppositions.[32] However, the question is also, to what extent the missionaries understood the meaning of the words they discovered in translation.

The missionaries' message was seldom swallowed wholesale by African converts. More often the message underwent a transformation based on creative appropriation. As a rule, the transformation was a subtle, internal one, but in the end, it resulted in outright rebellion against the white control of the message. The early Christian missionaries tended to view the local customs and traditions that they confronted as superstitious, reflecting an ignorant or backward cultural status. However, the revolts that met those who taught from this perspective demonstrate that taking such a view of things did not necessarily pay off. There were also exceptions from the condescending mainstream understanding of the missionaries, like Bishop Colenso and Johannes van der Kemp from the London Missionary Society, who both in different ways challenged the colonial paradigm of Western superiority.[33]

Missionary interventions produced a great number of new written languages and millions of readers. Their translations, based on the written word, were quite obviously a cultural achievement. However, the impact of this achievement was also to primitivize and tribalize peoples in their own histories, making them see their own pasts in superstitious terms. The legacy of the missionaries' engagement with the native languages is therefore ambiguous.[34]

The meaning of ubuntu in the minds of the missionaries

Gade scanned the digitized version of the Xhosa translation of the New Testament in 1846 and counted six mentions of *ubuntu*. This is the first documented reference of the use of *ubuntu* in written form. However, Gade did not investigate the translation work in detail. This chapter fills this gap. What was in the English and German minds of the translating missionaries? From what biblical context did they set out when looking for a Xhosa word?[35]

Henry Hare Dugmore from Birmingham, who belonged to the Eastern Cape Albany settlers, was one of two protagonists in the translation team. In 1820, aged ten, he accompanied his parents, when they emigrated from England after his father had become insolvent. At 14, Dugmore began a seven-year unpaid apprenticeship as a saddler. At 21 he was accepted into a Methodist priest and missionary seminary, and three years later, in 1834, he became a candidate for the Wesleyan ministry, appointed to Mount Coke where his supervisor encouraged him to develop his aptitude for languages. William Binnington Boyce from Yorkshire was another Wesleyan missionary in the Cape Colony. In 1830 he was sent to Buntingvale, Eastern Cape and tasked to write a grammar of the 'Kaffir' language, the Nguni language spoken in the Eastern Cape, today's Xhosa. (The term 'Kaffir' eventually drifted away from its original meanings – the Arabic meaning of infidel, and the British colonial meaning of Xhosa – and, under apartheid, came to be an extremely derogatory word for African people in general. Today, it is still highly offensive and classed as hate-speech.) Dugmore soon mastered W. B. Boyce's *Grammar of the Kaffir Language* published in 1834 and quickly became fluent in Xhosa.[36] In 1839 he was ordained into the Wesleyan ministry and became resident minister in Graham's Town (today's Grahamstown).

The following year, at the age of 26, John Whittle Appleyard came to the Eastern Cape, or British Kaffraria as it was called, as a Methodist missionary. There he met Dugmore. Appleyard was the second of the two protagonists of translating the work into Xhosa and the one who first came up with the idea. Behind this initiative was Robert Moffat's translation of the New Testament into Tswana in 1839. Moffat's translation was ground-breaking. It was the first African-language Bible, creating the way for dozens of other efforts to disseminate Christianity and spread literacy, among them the Xhosa New Testament in 1846.[37]

Moffat, born in Scotland in 1795, moved to England to find work as a gardener and a farmer. With his Methodist and Scottish Congregationalist sympathies he applied successfully to the London Missionary Society and was dispatched to

South Africa in 1816. In 1820, after three years in Namaqualand, an Atlantic coast region in the north of the Cape colony, he moved with his wife east to the Griqua Town, today Griekwastad, where their daughter Mary was born. (Mary would later become David Livingstone's wife.) What became a large family settled in the end at a mission station established at Kuruman, north of the Vaal River. From there Moffat made numerous journeys into neighbouring regions, going as far north as Matabeleland in today's Zimbabwe, from where he reported what he experienced to the Royal Geographic Society. His field report, 'Moffat, Missionary Labours and Scenes,' written and published after the completion of the Tswana New Testament translation during leave in England (1839–1843), documents these travels and life at the mission station. One might assume that Moffat was in England not only to rest and write up his history, but also to raise money. On the final pages of the book, in an enthusiastic panorama sketch on the future, he referenced the work of Thomas Fowell Buxton, the English MP, brewer and social reformer, who had advocated better prison conditions, a more humane criminal law and (following on from the abolition of slave trade in 1807) the abolition of slavery. Buxton had published his African Slave Trade the same year as Moffat published the Tswana New Testament. Their mutual task was to rescue Africa from the abyss of misery in which it had been plunged, Moffat stated, quoting Buxton.

In 1846, Dugmore, William J. Davis and Joseph Warner from the Wesleyan Missionary Society, along with Carl Wilhelm Posselt and Jakob Döhne from the Berlin Missionary Society, published *Itestamente Entsha Yenkosi Yetu Kayesu Kristu, Gokwamaxosa*, the first complete edition of the New Testament translated into Xhosa. It reached 442 unpaginated pages, printed in sections with the text in double-column format. The portions were printed at Fort Peddie and Emtati (Xhosa for Newton Dale). The printing had begun in 1842 and was completed in February 1846. This was the text where, as far as we know, *ubuntu* was written for the first time.[38]

Dugmore not only assisted Appleyard with allocating the work to various missionaries, but also undertook a general revision of the translations of the Psalms and Gospels together with Acts, Romans, Philippians, Colossians, Thessalonians, Titus, and Philemon. Beyond these translations, he also set Xhosa words to hymns and composed music. Appleyard seems to have concentrated on the Old Testament published in Xhosa in 1859. He was familiar with Hebrew, Greek, Latin, Dutch, and Xhosa. Dugmore's skill as a Xhosa linguist is testified. A British army officer complained that the missionaries in general spoke Xhosa grammatically, without learning the pronunciation and intonation as spoken by the Africans. Missionaries spoke and learnt the language in the manner white people learn languages, the officer complained, ignoring the fact that a word pronounced one way has one meaning but by giving it a different intonation or altering the prefix a totally opposite meaning may be given to it. This officer considered Dugmore to be unlike these missionaries. Dugmore was in great demand as an interpreter by the colonial authorities in their dealings with the Xhosa people.[39]

The most striking translation of *ubuntu* in the 1846 Xhosa translation is in the Book of Jude, the shortest book at the end of the New Testament just before the

Book of Revelations. The context is the denouncement of the sinful life in Sodom and Gomorra, Jude 1:7–8:

...ekela **ubuntu** bumbi,[40] zimi- siweke ukubangumzekeliso, zibuva ubuhlungu bomlilo o- bungunapakade. 8 Kanjalo ababapupi aba- ncolileyo bayancolisa **ubuntu**, bayadela ubukosi, bayateta okukohlakeleyo gamatshawe.

In the English Standard Version translation these verses run:

... just as Sodom and Gomorrah and the surrounding cities, which likewise indulged in sexual immorality and pursued **unnatural desire**, serve as an example by undergoing a punishment of eternal fire. Yet in like manner these people also, relying on their dreams, defile **the flesh**, reject authority, and blaspheme the glorious ones.

In the 1834 version of Luther's New Testament in German, the version which the German translators probably had as their point of departure, the wording is more drastic, cruder, indeed, fleshier:

Wie auch Sodom und Gomorra und die umliegenden Städte, die gleicher Weise, wie diese, **ausgehuret** haben, und nach einem andern Fleisch gegangen sind, ß.zmn Exempel gesetzet sind, und leiden des ewigen Feuers Pein. *Desselbigen gleichen sind auch diese Träumer, die **das Fleisch** beflecken, die Herr, schaflen aber verachten und die Majestäten listern.

A few verses later in the Book of Jude (16–17) *ubuntu* is used to translate 'favouritism': 'ncoma **ubuntu** ba- bantugenxa yenzuzo.' The origin in English of this translation is: 'they are loud-mouthed boasters, showing **favouritism** to gain advantage'; and in German: '*und ihr Mund redet stolze Worte, und achten das **Ansehen der Person** um Nutzes willen.*'

In Mark 12:14, *ubuntu* is used to translate 'swayed by appearances' (as opposed to 'truly teaching the way of God'), and in Romans 6:6–7 *ubuntu* stands for 'old self,' which was crucified; in German, '*alter Mensch.*' Finally, in Peter 3:18, 'flesh' is again the word that is translated with *ubuntu*.

The semantic field in which *ubuntu* was embedded was obviously quite different from the understanding of it today. The translators of the New Testament into Xhosa linked *ubuntu* to imperfect as opposed to perfect, human nature as opposed to divinity, flesh as opposed to spirit, body as opposed to soul, impure as opposed to pure, maculate as opposed to immaculate. This semantic embedding constituted the dark side of the Christian dichotomy of good and evil, a side that the Methodist and Pietist missionaries were keen to emphasize in the world-image they wanted to disseminate to the indigenous people. Even if it is important to take note of the fact that it was a rare concept in the translation, used only six times, and far from a key concept, its semantics and its distinct profile are nevertheless remarkable.

The question emerges of when and how the shift towards today's meaning began. On this question one might refer to Paul Landau's observation, mentioned above, about how the ambiguity of key words used by the missionaries sometimes led them to split the words in two, one meaning referring to the intended *replacement* of 'heathen beliefs,' and the other referring to exactly those 'heathen' practices that the missionaries wanted to replace. In the Christian doctrines, humankind connotes both the human as flesh and imperfect, and the human as God's creation and the bearer of God's image.

The selection of *ubuntu* departed from a Manichean Christian imaginary of divinity and holiness as opposed to earthliness and sinfulness, of the ideal of perfection and the reality of human imperfection. The problem was how to communicate key concepts in a religious imaginary unknown to the receivers of the message, how to pick a native word that could translate this idea in an understandable way. For this purpose, the missionaries needed to build language bridges.

The question is how the missionary team around Dugmore came to pick *ubuntu* when they searched for a term meaning adultery and sin. One possibility is that they were wrong and that they did not master Xhosa. We have seen Moffat's account of all the difficulties and traps that led to shortcomings in translation work. Still, the question mark around the exclusively negative connotation of *ubuntu* in the 1846 Xhosa translation remains. Moffat's 1839 Tswana New Testament translation was, as we have seen, the pioneering work in Biblical translations to local languages in South Africa. He, too, was a highly esteemed language expert. The Xhosa word *ubuntu* is *botho* in Tswana. Do the six references to *ubuntu* in the 1846 Xhosa translation draw on *botho* in the 1839 Tswana translation?[41] Is there any similarity between the two translations that suggests Moffat's influence?

The first mentions of *ubuntu* in Xhosa in Jude are stand-ins for 'unnatural desire' and 'flesh,' translated respectively as *mokgwa wa nama e sele* and as *nama*. *Nama* deals with 'sin' in the understanding of the word today. What it meant in pre-Christian times (when it lacked an equivalence to religious sin) is difficult to know. *Mokgwa wa nama e sele* means 'a practice of fleshly things.' *Nana* bears no relation to *botho*, and *botho* would not make sense in this context. The phrase *Ba tlhaola batho*, used in Jude 1:16 for 'showing favouritism,' has nothing to do with *botho*. There is no relation between *batho* and *botho*. The same is true for *bonman yoa batho* as this appears in Mark. The use of *ubuntu* for 'flesh' in the First Epistle of Peter is not translated with *botho* in Tswana, but rather with *namen*. Only the translation of 'self' in Romans refers to *botho*. 'Self' is the most neutral of the six negative connotations of *ubuntu* in the Xhosa translation. This is where the Tswana translation uses *botho*. The rest of the translation uses different words from *botho*, giving it a negative meaning much like that of the Xhosa translation.

The translating missionaries gave *ubuntu* a new meaning in their outline of a new religion, portraying humans both as apostasy and as divine copy. The indigenous population did not think in these categories. *Ubuntu* was probably a neutral concept. The missionaries loaded it with the negative meaning of humans being defective and imperfect. This is the opposite of the meaning of *ubuntu* today. The question is when the shift towards a more positive connotation began. Gade, in his pioneering mapping of the occurrence of *ubuntu* in nineteenth- and twentieth-century texts, finds the first reference after the 1846 Xhosa New Testament in 1850. He does not provide closer analysis, however. He merely records that *ubuntu* was translated as 'human nature' by Appleyard, the Wesleyan missionary and friend of Dugmore.[42] Going a bit deeper into this source than Gade, who has used a more quantitative approach in mapping the origin of *ubuntu*, reveals interesting details. Ten years after his arrival in the Eastern Cape, and, as we saw, after having handed over the idea of a Xhosa Biblical translation to Dugmore, Appleyard published his book on the Xhosa language, where he comments on *ubuntu* in a section which begins, 'Diminutive Nouns: More generally... a different prefix causes a different signification to the same root.' Hence: *umntu*, human being; *isintu*, human species; *uluntu*, human race; *ubuntu*, human nature.[43]

'Human nature' fits *per se* with the missionaries' use of *ubuntu* in the 1846 New Testament translation, in the sense that there is a potential but not necessarily actual connotation of imperfection in the term. In a non-Christian heuristic framework 'human nature' is a neutral term. It takes on negative meaning within Christian semantics. The 'old self,' as Dugmore translated it, fits well with human nature in a negative sense, for instance. However, the translation of the term in 1850 is more neutral than in the 1846 Xhosa New Testament, with human nature no longer necessarily implying a defect. It is a translation fit for a dictionary, rather than a religious Christian text. It is made by a missionary, but in an act of translation *from* the local language into English. The missionaries who translated the New Testament into Xhosa worked in the opposite direction. They were looking for a word in Xhosa that corresponded to the English or German words they had in mind. Overall, it seems that the translators of the New Testament into Xhosa added negative meaning, making new sense of the concept, a new sense connected to a new imaginary of religion and transcendental thought as well as a new world-image at variance with vernacular modes of interpreting the world. *Ubuntu* was once more given a somewhat more neutral twist in the 1850 grammar.

Gade registers the occurrence of *ubuntu* in a Zulu-to-English grammar (1855) and dictionary (1861) by Colenso. Here it is also rewarding to go deeper into the conceptual history of the word. Colenso was Anglican bishop of Natal from 1853. His *Elementary Grammar of the Zulu-Kafir Language: Prepared for the Use of Missionaries, and Other Students* taught that 'the original form of the inflex *um* or *u* was *umu*, and that in some Zulu words the sound of the second u might still be heard. Thus *umu-Ti* for tree and *umu-Ntu* for man.'[44] He then gives examples of the use of *umuntu*. *Umu-Ntu o n' ama Nhla* means 'the man with strength = strong man' and *umu Ntuo hambayo* is 'a man who is a walker = a wanderer.'[45] *Umu Ntu mu-ñe* is translated with 'one man' and *omu-ñe UmuNtu* with 'another man, a second man.'[46] *UmuNtu iliZwe lake li n'aman Hla* means 'the man whose word is powerful' and *UmuNtu o'n Hliziyo im-bi* 'the man whose heart (is) bad.'[47] *UmiNtu muni*? means 'which man?,' *umuNtu* means 'person,' and *gaba ngumuNtu* means 'it is probably a man.'

Colenso's 1861 Zulu–English dictionary has an extensive entry for *ubuntu*:

NTU (*Umu*), n. Any personal being; person, human being; specially, a native, man, woman, or child; dependent of a chief; used of a humane, kind-hearted person. Ex. *Umuntu*, another man, *abuntu*, other people, *abantu*, the people = the natives.

Umuntu wesilisa, wesifana, man, woman.
Umuntu o umuntu, a true man, humane
Umuntu onge'muntu, one not worthy the name of man
NTU (Isi), n. Human race, mankind.[48]

In Colenso's translation of *ubuntu* in the 1861 Zulu dictionary there is little trace of the semantic field by which the term became embedded in the Xhosa New Testament of 1846. The same goes for the 1855 grammar. The only connection there to the 1846 text is the composition 'the man whose heart is bad,' but that meaning is not for *ubuntu* as such but rather appears in a construction with other words. In the 1861 dictionary there is the direct meaning of kind-hearted person. The general meaning in Colenso's use of *ubuntu* is neutral to positive, and the meaning varies between a human as an individual and humans as humankind.

How should one understand this displacement of meaning in 10–15 years? The knowledge of the Nguni languages might have increased in a time of expanding colonialism and missionary enterprises in the Cape, an increase that might have led to more possibilities for translation. The missionaries might have experienced the negative connotation of *ubuntu* not making sense when they disseminated the new religion. It is difficult to attain any precise understanding of these hypothetical possibilities during a time when a translation to and from a spoken language did not benefit from the availability of written texts. There was no written documentation or expounding of the etymology of the term to draw on. There was no dictionary the missionaries could use in order to understand the meaning of the words of the African languages.

However, possibly a more important factor is who the translator was, and from what church or theological school he came. The Wesleyan Methodists and the German Pietists around Dugmore possessed a more Manichean worldview and emphasized the issue of sin more than the Anglican bishop. They loaded *ubuntu* with negative meaning. Colenso, like the Methodist Reverend Appleyard was born in 1814. He came to the Cape Colony in 1853, 13 years after Appleyard. After the financial bankruptcy of his father, Colenso grew up in precarious circumstances. He had a peripatetic life as a mathematical student and tutor. He was an usher (assistant teacher) at a private school and a sizar (undergraduate receiving financial help for menial duties) at Cambridge before he studied theology and became a missionary. However, these hermeneutical discrepancies reflected not only a difference in terms of exegetics between different churches and theological doctrines but also between individuals. Colenso had a more liberal interpretation of Christendom in which sin was not as central as a concept as it was for the Methodists. Colenso was the first Church of England bishop in Natal. He was more than a theologian, philologist, and translator, however. He was also a social activist with politically as well as theologically radical opinions and reckoned to be controversial. His theology was radical in a very different sense than that of the Wesleyans. He opposed the doctrine of eternal punishment and challenged the argument that the communion was a precondition for salvation. He also denied that the ancestors of recently Christianized native Africans were condemned to eternal damnation. One might understand the different approaches to *ubuntu* as an interpretative struggle among the missionaries over assigning meaning to a native concept in the dissemination of a religious message from contentious theological perspectives.

The encounter with indigenous culture and customs, and his dealings with the locals who visited his mission station, in terms of questions about what to believe and how to live, made Colenso rethink biblical texts. His critical questioning of the literal understanding of parts of the Pentateuch and the Book of Joshua, and his suggestion that these texts should rather be understood historically, led to a scandal in England. His plea for polygenism did not make him less controversial. This belief in polygenism, or 'CoAdamism' as he called it, underpinned his theological proclivity to confront doctrines and established truths. Colenso argued that the human race had sprung from more than one couple, that is, from more than one Adam and Eve, and he argued that monogenesis was the cause of racism and slavery. Each race had sprung from different pairs of parents and all races had been created equal by God. Against the backdrop of his theory of polygenism, Colenso also advocated polygamy for 'converts from heathenism.'[49]

It is here important to emphasize that he was not an advocate of polygamy in general terms but only for those converts who already practiced polygamy. His point was that polygamy should not be an obstacle to conversion. His many adversaries among white people in general, and the church establishment in particular, failed in their campaign to remove Colenso from his episcopal chair but succeeded in restricting his freedom to preach. Colenso also had to endure a dubious excommunication and the consecration of a rival bishop in Pietermaritzburg.[50]

Colenso and the group around Dugmore had strongly divergent theological approaches, and it would be reasonable to assume that that would be reflected in the shift in the meaning of *ubuntu* that occurred after the Xhosa version of the New Testament in 1846. However, in the book on the Zulu language by Appleyard a few years later, the translation of *ubuntu*, in line with Colenso's grammar and dictionary, indicates that a broader and more neutral understanding emerged in the expanding contacts between the colonizers and the colonized. However, the direction of translation, from or to the local language, might also have played a role. The zealous desire to impose a message could well be stronger when translating into the local language than from it, when the focus would be on learning rather than teaching.

The concept of *ubuntu* was by no means a key concept that played a major role in the language of the missionaries. The differences in meaning of *ubuntu* between the Methodist and Pietist translators of the New Testament into Xhosa in 1846, and the Anglican bishop Colenso in his grammar and Zulu–English dictionary 9 and 15 years respectively later, nevertheless suggest that the understanding of *ubuntu* reflected different theological approaches, where Colenso was less Manichean and more open to syncretism and multicultural views. Colenso's translation deprived *ubuntu* of the theological meaning that the translators of the 1846 Xhosa New Testament had given it. In other words, the Xhosa translation in 1846 did not make the theological sense that the missionaries believed it did. One should here also pay attention to Moffat's much more differentiated translation into Tswana in 1839, when he used other words than *botho* to express negative meaning and uses *botho* only once.

74 Ubuntu *as religion, as law, and as politics*

Figure 3.1 Missionaries searching for words in languages without letters to translate their message. Fr left John Whittle Appleyard (above), Henry Hare Dugmore (below), Robert Moffat, John William Colenso. Copyrights: Appleyard: public domain, Dugmore: Wiki Commons/Creative Commons (https://commons.wikimedia.org/wiki/File:HenryHareDugmore(ca.1890).jpg, Moffat: George Baxter, Robert Moffat © National Portrait Gallery, London, Colenso: Unknown photographer, John William Colenso © National Portrait Gallery, London.

From a concept for sin to the language of emancipation and a critique of apartheid

In his text scanning, Gade found that, during the century after the missionaries' translations, *ubuntu* did not occur very frequently and that it hardly had any particularly positive or negative flavour. He found 31 texts before 1950 that contain the term *ubuntu*. Before 1980 it was translated as 'human nature,' 'humanity,' 'humanness,' 'humaneness,' 'human feeling,' 'real humanity,' 'human kindness,' 'manhood,' 'goodness of nature,' 'good moral disposition,' 'virtue,' 'the sense of common humanity,' 'true humanity,' 'true good fellowship and sympathy in joy and sorrow,' 'reverence for human nature,' 'essential humanity,' 'the kindly simple feeling for persons as persons,' 'manliness,' 'liberality,' 'a person's own human nature,' 'generosity,' 'good disposition,' 'good moral nature,' 'personhood,' 'personality,' 'politeness,' 'kindness,' 'a feeling of human wellbeing,' 'the characteristic of being truly human,' 'greatness of soul,' and the 'capacity of social self-sacrifice on behalf of others.'[51]

As opposed to the first missionary translation of *ubuntu* in 1846, the concept acquires a more positive meaning, but also becomes more open and vaguer. It loses distinction. Before the 1950s, all written sources referring to *ubuntu* were authored by people of European descent. Alexis Kagame, a Rwandan historian, philosopher, and Catholic priest from the Tutsi group, was the first African to publish a text mentioning *ubuntu* in Gade's sample. In a book in French on the philosophy of being in Bantu-Rwanda he translated *ubuntu* to *libéralité*. Between 1957 and 1960 Archibald Campbell Jordan, a Xhosa novelist and teacher, wrote a series of articles under the heading of 'Towards an African Literature.' Gade suggests that his article entitled 'Literary Stabilization,' originally from the October–December 1957 issue of *Africa South*, and Chapter 6 of *Towards an African Literature*, may be the first text authored by a *South African* of African descent that contains the term '*ubuntu*': 'The converted has lost *ubuntu* (generosity, respect for man irrespective of position). The pagan can no longer expect hospitality amongst the Christians.'[52] Jordan was born at a mission station in today's Eastern Cape province as the son of an Anglican Church minister. He was trained as a teacher and became president of the African Teachers' Association, and he started his writing career with the publication of poetry in the newspaper *Imvo Zabantsundu*. He also started work on his classic Xhosa novel, *Ingqumbo Yezinyanya*, which was published in 1940 and translated decades later into English as *The Wrath of the Ancestors*.

Another early African writer who used the concept of *ubuntu* as a potentially emancipatory concept was Jordan Kush Ngubane, who studied at Adams College, near Durban. Because of increasing racial pressures, he moved his family to Swaziland in 1962, where he farmed a modest property and occasionally wrote, through which he became one of the most prominent Zulu intellectuals. He mentioned *ubuntu* in writing from the 1950s in the magazine *Drum*, which was intended for a black readership and known for its reports on urban African culture in the 1950s and 1960s. The heyday of the magazine was between the 1952 Defiance Campaign, the first large-scale multiracial political mobilization against apartheid, and the 1960

Sharpeville massacre. Ngubane worked closely with the Zulu chief Albert Luthuli, teacher, activist, and politician, from 1940 until Luthuli was awarded the Nobel Peace Prize in 1960 for his 'non-violent struggle against apartheid.' Ngubane's novel *Uvalo Lwezinhlonzi* ('His Frowns Struck Terror', 1957), was popular when it appeared and was even a required school text before being banned from 1962 to 1967. His nonfiction works included *An African Explains Apartheid* (1963) and *Conflict of Minds* (1979). In 1979 he also published a study in which he compared the racial issues in the United States to those in South Africa.

In the 1950s, and reinforced in the 1960s and 1970s, *ubuntu* slowly began to take on political meaning. It became somewhat more frequently used, without becoming a very strong political concept. A decade or two after the 1846 translation, the early theologization of the term, initially with a negative connotation, began to acquire a secular meaning with a positive inflexion, although with an associated vagueness as to its meaning, as we saw. It remained a concept at that level for a century. From the 1950s onwards, the universalism associated with the term began to shift towards Africanism, towards a concept describing African humanism, philosophy, and ethics (dignity), and in so doing to align itself with a worldview centred on Africa. Native African writers began to refer to *ubuntu* as a particular African value. The sense of the word was positive, as discussion of the concept came to be seen as a potential instrument of political emancipation. A slight and

Figure 3.2 A C Jordan (left) and J K Ngubane. African intellectuals working on an African literature and culture referring to *ubuntu*. Copyrights and sources: Jordan: University of Wisconsin-Madison Archives Photo Collection, Box 75, Folder 3/1 Jordan, Dr. A. C.; Ngubane: DISA archives (https://disa.ukzn.ac.za/sites/default/files/pdf_files/Ctv4n261.pdf). Photo from a cover of *The Contact Journal* published by the Liberal Party of South Africa ©.

slow politicization of the concept began, and although *ubuntu* was not a widely invoked or strongly galvanizing concept, it nevertheless became an emerging concept of political relevance.

A case in point is the constitution of the Inkatha Freedom Party (IFP). Chief Mangosuthu (Gatsha) Buthelezi, a former member of the ANC Youth League, established the Inkatha National Cultural Liberation Movement, which in 1975 became the IFP. In 1976, the apartheid regime appointed Buthelezi government chief in the Kwa Zulu region in Natal, considered autonomously African by the regime. As opposed to the ANC, he refused armed resistance against apartheid. Despite the intense and volatile relationship between the IFP and the ANC, which occasionally descended into bitter enmity and an awful power struggle with thousands of death victims, they were somehow united in their common struggle against apartheid. Inkatha, meaning 'crown' in Zulu, was originally a cultural association for Zulus founded in the 1920s by the Zulu king Solomon kaDinuzulu. Buthelezi used the Inkatha movement to promote Zulu nationalism. This did not necessarily correspond to the ANC's aims, which led to the ANC branding Buthelezi a counter-revolutionary. The Inkatha movement embodied contradictions and so did Buthelezi, who died in 2023 at 1995. His contested personality gave him characteristics like a bearer of hope and a freedom fighter as well as a henchman and a follower of the apartheid regime. The basis of his political ambition was the fact that the traditional Zulu leadership was dependent on the apartheid regime for its privileged status. However, it is not his controversial personality that makes him relevant in this chapter but the fact that he made *ubuntu* a political key concept in the Inkatha movement. At the founding congress of the IFP in 1975, the approved constitution of the party referred to *ubuntu* at a time when the ANC had not started using it:

> Accepting the fact that we have many things to copy from Western economic, political and education [*sic*] patterns of development, and striving for the promotion of African pattern [*sic*] of thought and the achievement of African Humanism otherwise commonly known in Nguni languages as UBUNTU and in Sotho languages as Botho: EMBRACING the principles of African humanism otherwise known as *Ubuntu/Botho* and accepting that governments are instituted and maintained to promote and protect human dignity, personal growth and fulfilment, and the individual pursuit of happiness.[53]

In 1980, there were signs that the development of a politicization of the concept of *ubuntu* was taking off when, against the backdrop of the end of white minority rule in Zimbabwe earlier that year, Stanlake and Tommie Marie Samkange, published the book *Hunhuism or Ubuntuism: A Zimbabwe Indigenous Political Philosophy*.[54] *Hunhu/ubuntu* was the concept on which to build a new Zimbabwean identity, they argued. The book outlined an indigenous political philosophy for a new era that was distinct from liberalism, socialism, communism, and other Western ideologies. Stanlake Samkange was a Zimbabwean author, journalist, teacher, historian, and Africanist. He was an activist and at times a politician deeply involved in liberal politics in South Africa in the 1950s and 1960s. With his wife Tommie

Marie (Anderson) Samkange, a black American psychologist, whom he met in Indiana during his master studies in the 1950s, they became a prominent intellectual couple. They moved back to the USA disappointed and disillusioned about the prospects of a multicultural Rhodesia. They returned in 1978 engaging themselves in African nationalist politics and intellectual debate. When the independence of Zimbabwe stood clear in 1979, Stanlake withdrew from politics concentrating on his writing. They didn't write just *Hunhuism and Ubuntuism* together but also other books such as *African Saga* (1971), a history of Africa.

This development, which happened at the tail end of 400 years of colonialism, shone a particular light on the recently intensified apartheid politics in South Africa. Europe and Africa, white and black, became more thematized in terms of alternative power and separation, but of a very different kind than that which the

Figure 3.3 Stanlake Samkange. *Drum* published this photo in March 1979 with the following text: Stanlake's Castle – A proud Stanlake with his mansion and Rolls-Royce. "They felt it's not just my car but their car, too," he says of his old township friends. Professor Stanlake Samkange is hardly a newcomer to the jungle-like politics of Rhodesia. At 56, one must assume he knows what he's up to when he parades himself, his 17-year-old son, Stan, two dogs and a 1965 Silver Cloud Rolls-Royce in front of a mock medieval castle set deep in the heart of Hatfield, a once all-White Salisbury suburb. Had the professor been a member of the Zambian ruling hierarchy of Dr Kenneth Kaunda, hardly a soul would have batted an eyelid. Photograph by *Drum* photographer © BAHA.

apartheid regime had in mind. Established power relationships began to be challenged. Africans began to search for their African origin with the goal of replacing white power with black power.

Post-apartheid: ubuntu for reconciliation

After the collapse of the Soviet Union and the end of the Cold War around 1990, the international isolation of South Africa's apartheid regime grew. The 'communist threat,' which the apartheid regime had said it was fighting, no longer existed. The South African government was deprived of the main reason for its oppression of the non-white population and its aggressive foreign policy in Namibia, Angola and elsewhere. The regime's economy added to its problems. Since the 1980s, pressure had been felt from international sanctions and high unemployment figures amongst the black population. The latter led to growing black resistance on the labour markets. The power of the white minority was declining. After the liberal global triumph, the regime looked around for an exit.

In February 1990, the leader of the regime, F. W. de Klerk, announced the release of Nelson Mandela from his Robben Island prison and legalized the ANC and all other banned organizations. Mandela had been sentenced to life imprisonment in the Rivonia Trial in 1964 and, from his cell, became the symbol of the resistance to apartheid. 'Free Mandela' was a world-wide cry. Time had come for negotiations on future cohabitation based on new perspectives, de Klerk declared. The ANC could no longer rely on the Soviet Union for support and saw an interest in negotiations, too.

The negotiations were difficult and accompanied by violence. Strong tensions emerged between the ANC and the IFP. Ethnic conflicts erupted, such as the Boipatong massacre in June 1992, when IFP fighters attacked a Gauteng township, killing 45 and leading to ANC accusations against the police and their withdrawal from the negotiations. In addition to Black-on-Black violence, there were attacks on white civilians, and white right-wing violence added to multilateral hostilities. The negotiations were resumed, however, and in 1993 de Klerk and Mandela were jointly awarded the Nobel Peace Prize. In the same year, a temporary constitution was settled.

Violence, including car bomb attacks, persisted right up to the first general elections on 27 April 1994, but the elections, during which 20 million South Africans cast their votes, were peaceful. At midnight the new six-colour flag was raised to the strains of the old national anthem *Die Stem van Suid-Afrika* (The Call of South Africa) and the new one, *Nkosi Sikelel' iAfrika* (God Bless Africa). Henceforth, it was intended that they would be co-official, but in 1997, they were merged and extended with new English lyrics.

The ANC won 62.65 percent of the votes, just a little less than the two thirds it needed to rewrite the temporary constitution alone. Negotiations had to continue. The violence that had accompanied the march to the new South Africa made reconciliation an imperative for both black and white leaders. The realization developed that there could be no new start without reconciliation. Nelson Mandela personified

80 Ubuntu *as religion, as law, and as politics*

these feelings more than anybody else. This was the situation in which *ubuntu* emerged as a galvanizing and unifying key concept. Drucilla Cornell and her team have explored this development.⁵⁵

As we saw in Chapter 1, *ubuntu* connoted progress and a breakthrough from the old system towards a new one, although it saw progress less in an economic, material sense and more in an ethical and normative sense concerned with moral betterment. The appeal of reconciliation was its call for consensus rather than conflict, for value commonality and community rather than competition. As well as its political appeal, it had a strong legal one, too. The new South African courts were eager to connect their dispensation of justice to the new meta-norm.

Tom Bennett has investigated the connection between the legal system and the norm of *ubuntu* in detail in several works, most recently, *Ubuntu: An African Jurisprudence*.⁵⁶ He highlights the role of the constitutional revolution in the early 1990s that triggered a rapid reception of *ubuntu* into the legal system. Once nonwhite Africans were given full equality with other members of the population and discrimination based on race was abandoned, there was the potential to give institutions of African customary law greater prominence, and suggestions were made to merge common and customary law into one system. But these proposals never

Figure 3.4 Nelson Mandela casting his vote in the 1994 elections, the first time he voted in his life. The photo was taken at Ohlange School, Inanda, Durban, by the Independent Electoral Commission's official photographer, Paul Weinberg.

resulted in concrete agreements. Customary law continued to be separated from British-Dutch common law, although its position was upgraded. It was not because of a major redesign, or the Africanization of the legal system that the language of *ubuntu* gained adherence in the early 1990s. The concept began to permeate the legal system almost incidentally before it set about its political and ideological purpose of creating national unity. It became a legal doctrine supporting its own discourse in South African law which, however, in principle remains dual (common and customary).[57]

Adopting *ubuntu* into South African law can be seen as an epilogue to the interim constitution in 1993 under the rubric of National Unity and Reconciliation and was intended to be a set of moral guidelines of little legal weight. *Ubuntu* appeared again in 1995, in the preamble of the Promotion of National Unity and Reconciliation Act, which established a Truth and Reconciliation Commission (TRC) to negotiate the past and settle historical injustices. In the same year, Augustine Shutte, philosopher and theologian at the University of Cape Town, launched the Common Good Project, coinciding with the publication of a new edition of his book, *Philosophy for Africa*, which introduced *ubuntu* as 'something of great value we can offer to the rest of the world.' He revived the general saying, *umuntu ngamuntu ngabantu*, 'a person is a person through other people,' and argued that the constitutional framework of South Africa would require a sense of community and caring for fellow human beings.[58]

A legal definition of *ubuntu* was as hard to come by as the political one. On the one hand, law avoids technical terms with open-ended meanings, although on the other hand certain terms are allowed to remain ambiguous to permit courts discretion in applying them to diverse situations. 'Wrongful' and 'reasonable' are typical words of the latter variety. *Ubuntu* is another example. Judges, practitioners, and academics have filled many pages to define it in a way that does not impair the overall purpose of using it. In fact, as Bennett argues, to impose boundaries on the scope of the term, and restrict its semantic range, would be ill-advised at a time of transformative constitutionalism in South Africa in which *ubuntu* played a critical role.[59]

One way to try to stabilize its abundance of meaning has been to compare it with other legal terms such as equity, dignity, and equality. A related discussion deals with the question of whether, in relation to such terms, *ubuntu* represents values of an African origin or whether it also connotes Western, enlightenment values. There is, for instance, in *ubuntu*, a dimension of dignity that reminds one of Kant. Both *ubuntu* and Kantian philosophy possess a common concern with freedom and morality, obligation and necessity, which allows them to converge as ethical ideals. Theological perspectives have supported such thinking, although they derive the ethical ideal from God. Ranged against the voices that have emphasized a significant degree of overlap between *ubuntu* and Kantian dignity, however, are others who have underlined the differences.[60]

Tom Bennett, in his exploration of the legal side of the spread of the *ubuntu* vocabulary, takes note of the initial hesitancy in the reception of the concept. It was considered to be nothing but an academic construct, an attempt to call to life a spirit

82 Ubuntu *as religion, as law, and as politics*

that was no longer alive, superfluous to a legal system already amply equipped with equitable principles and fundamental rights. Despite such initial voices, *ubuntu* was soon welcomed by scholars not only in law but also in other disciplines because of the political role that the concept played in bringing to the law distinctively African ideas of right-doing and decision-making.[61]

Ubuntu was a key word in the work of the TRC, and from there it was appropriated by courts and scholars for the introduction of African values to further the transformation of the legal order. Although the constitutional change entailed a decisive break with apartheid, it did not abruptly break with all past laws. Bennett emphasizes the transformative rather than revolutionary nature of this development. Parliament sought to spearhead this development, but the government could not immediately attend to all demands, and when new laws were promulgated, ambiguities and loopholes remained, which necessitated the involvement of the courts in this transformation.[62]

Ubuntu as a legal concept does not have an all-encompassing power like the Bill of Rights. Its main function is rather to modify, correct or supplement the effects of the plain letter of the law. *Ubuntu* has a legal function that neither common-law

Figure 3.5 Desmond Tuti chaired the Truth and Reconciliation Commission, 1986-1996 Anglican archbishop of Cape Town, 1984 Nobel Peace Prize laureate for his human rights activism. South African Embassy Washington D C 8 September 1997. © John Mathew Smith 2001.

equitable principles nor the Bill of Rights can perform. It imbues the legal order with an African set of values, thereby emphasizing South Africa's cultural and historical framework from a post-apartheid viewpoint. In this respect *ubuntu* played an important role in the post-apartheid transformation of the legal system. Bennett also raised the question of how far the concept can assist in the continued need for transformation:

> In the second half of the 2010s, this question was given an acute urgency by radical student movements demanding a thorough decolonization of the law and the way in which it was taught. They claimed that, for far too long, traditional African learning and knowledge had been ignored, because of the racist and Eurocentric bias of South Africa's legal and educational systems. The students therefore demanded a more inclusive legal culture.[63]

This is a question that tightly connects *ubuntu* as a legal concept to *ubuntu* as a political concept. Of course, legal and political here are not separate, but rather two sides of the same thing. As a meta-norm, *ubuntu* gained a political as well as a legal appeal. In political terms, *ubuntu* became more elusive than it was during the years in which the apartheid regime was first being dismantled. The idea of reconciliation as the basis of political progress towards a new society of newly defined equals had an obvious galvanizing impact in the 1990s. However, in its relationship to reconciliation, it became overloaded with meaning and more generic, which in the end meant dilution of meaning and precision. Dismantling the apartheid regime was not the same thing as dismantling apartheid. The insight grew that there were continuities in the discontinuities. *Ubuntu's* loss of meaning as a political concept forfeits its sustainability and legitimacy as a legal one.

The anti-neoliberal defiance and the new politics of social distribution

The question of political legitimacy and sustainability leads to the question of a viable political economy, which was not a theme in the *ubuntu* discourse. For long-term credibility, the meta-norm required politics and institutions to promote decreasing social and racial inequalities. That was the implicit price by the white minority for forgiving and moving on. The elections in 1994 and the transition to a racially inclusive democracy triggered promises and hopes of decreased inequality. The winning slogan of the ANC election campaign promised a better life for all. The party's Reconstruction and Development Program (RDP) sought to alleviate poverty and deprivation and assured poor South Africans that it would empower them to seize opportunities to develop their full potential. On the one hand, this had a neoliberal undertone with the emphasis on empowerment through equal opportunities rather than social equality as such. On the other hand, the program had a kind of Keynesian welfarist subtext that was anything but mainstream in the world at the time of hegemonic neoliberalism. Housing subsidies for the poor were introduced and the welfare system in general was extended and embedded in a developmental discourse. Public works and land reform programs were launched, and credit schemes for the poor were introduced to encourage entrepreneurship. The

1996 constitution guaranteed socio-economic rights. The success of these measures seemed to be confirmed as, according to various gauges, poverty declined.[64]

Beyond the debate about to what extent the government executed neoliberal policies, the new South Africa became a pioneer and a model in other African countries through its expansion of social protection. South Africa led the way with an extensive national system of social payments for old-age pensioners, childcare grants, disability payments, and so on. Others in the region followed suit. James Ferguson describes a remarkable set of events that led to the sustained expansion of social assistance programs and the emergence of the contours of a new kind of welfare state. Against the many influential accounts of neoliberalism that tell of ever-growing social exclusion, one must "also take stock of a new kind of inclusion as millions of poor citizens previously ignored or worse by the state... [became] direct beneficiaries of cash payments."[65]

James Ferguson recognized that the anti-neoliberal critique got a lot right but pointed out that it was most articulate in what it was against. The politics of 'anti' did not constitute or consolidate identities by concrete programs of government or political mobilization *for* something but by declaration of opposition to what was wrong, building up a 'malevolent and polymorphic' Other.[66] Active opposition confirmed this Other; anti-neoliberalism cemented neoliberalism. Critical accounts of South Africa's neoliberalism failed to see the substantial and pioneering ways in which, at variance with the neoliberal model, the South-African government developed "an enormous system of non-contributory social benefits" that, in the early 2010s, transferred 3.4 percent of the nation's GNP directly to 'the poor' via non-market cash payments" and were received by more than 30 percent of the entire population.[67]

This development was not the product of an economic theory but of a quite particular conjuncture at the moment when the post-apartheid ANC regime came to power with a mandate to transform the economic conditions of the poor and working-class people who constituted its political base.

> Facing the pressing political need to deliver concrete changes to the new black political majority, and with 'pro-market' economic policies failing to yield the rapid economic growth that had been supposed to 'lift all boats', social protection became a key domain of policy innovation.[68]

South Africa and other countries in the region had long, well-developed social welfare systems for whites. Facing the changed neoliberal circumstances after apartheid, which called for balancing political expectations with economic constraints, the government did what it felt it had to do without asking about what the dominant neoliberal theory of the time prescribed. It equalized pension rates across racial groups and made social assistance available for much larger segments of the population. Along with this, it set up or radically extended the reach of national cash benefits. An intuitive grasp of what the situation called for rather than economic theory motivated political action.

The South African politics of social distribution had the potential to link up with an ethos of *ubuntu* for mutually reinforcing economic and political dynamics. However, after the Mandela years, the development went in another direction.

In a contradictory way, the generally positive indications of economic progress since 1994 contrast with negative assessments by South African as well as foreign observers. Apartheid did not die, and the poor rose in protest in the streets and through new social movements. Those seeking to understand the deeper causes for the emergence of widespread protest in the post-apartheid period have argued that the racialized inequities of apartheid had become new market inequities. The small, middle-class, black elite that existed under apartheid grew in number and accumulated more wealth, and some even became spectacularly rich, rising far above the middle-class category without necessarily demonstrating a deep, practical concern for those still languishing in poverty.

Despite the Growth, Employment and Redistribution program in 1996, and the expansion of the black empowerment program, critical voices increased within the Tripartite Alliance that had been forged in 1990 between the ANC, the trade union movement, and the communist party. They argued that Thabo Mbeki, who, since 1999 had been Mandela's successor, had adopted neoliberal politics. The tension between Mbeki and the left wing of the ANC grew. Vice president Jacob Zuma was one of those leftist critics. He was removed from his position but returned as Mbeki's successor in 2008. However, as president, he became the face of corruption disappointing those who had believed his promise to implement alternatives to neoliberalism. The Zuma presidency highlighted corruption and accusations of state capture, with the Gupta and Eskom scandals as the tip of the iceberg.

The development shows how difficult it was to remain unaffected by the neoliberal whirlwind in South Africa as well as Tanzania and elsewhere, despite the best intentions. The scope of national governments shrank unrelentingly. The freed financial markets punished budget deficits and imposed austerity politics. The ANC sharply experienced the difference between being a resistance movement and a party which leads the state.

According to a growing choir of social scientists, politicians and political activists, neoliberal ideology remained the cause of persistent poverty and inequality. They argued that, in 1996, when the ANC had effectively abandoned the RDP (despite some formal continuity) and adopted the Growth, Employment and Redistribution (GEAR) strategy, they had moved from a pro-poor to a pro-business, neoliberal approach. GEAR prioritized trade liberalization, the privatization of state-owned enterprises, fiscal austerity and 'reforms' in the labour market that were tailored to attracting investors. In the short term, the economy experienced deindustrialization, falling rates of formal employment and deepening poverty. The real value of the old-age pension and other social benefit programs declined. For this reason, the Communist Party, and, later, the trade unions, denounced GEAR as 'the 1996 class project.'[69]

Over the course of the 2000s, protests against the commodification of public services occurred. The protesters insisted that, although citizens had become consumers, they were unprotected when, for example, they fell into arrears paying for electricity or water, or repaying their mortgages.[70] Although at the national level, loyalty to the ANC remained in place, there were also protests against local-level ANC councillors. After 2012 when the leader of the ANC Youth League, Julius Malema, was kicked out of the party after he accused the ANC leadership of the extravagant consumption of luxury goods, the promotion of state-driven corruption and personal enrichment, the level of protests grew. After his exclusion, Malema, himself a massive and conspicuous consumer, initiated a campaign in which he restyled himself as the defender of the poor and ended up forming a new party, The Economic Freedom Fighters.

The anti-neoliberalist agenda in the South-African protest movement has confirmed and cemented the imaginary of neoliberalism as the predominant feature of the South African economy. The year 1994 was the apotheosis of a development that raised expectations but which, after a few years, morphed into disappointment. Deep contradictions have revealed a society plunged into turmoil. Since 1994, South African elections have confirmed the ANC's legitimacy and power, though both are declining. Simultaneously, the country has a high rate of protest and dissent in the workplace, the townships, universities, clinics, and central city squares. The level of political and criminal violence is alarming, and it becomes increasingly hard to disentangle the criminal from the political. The Marikana massacre of 2012 saw South African policemen shooting and killing 34 and injuring 78 striking miners, all employers of the British platinum producer Lonmin. This catastrophe, almost 20 years after the end of apartheid, activated memories of the Sharpeville massacre in 1960.

Reconciliation glossed over

The Marikana massacre reminds us that violence permeates South African history, the most infamous chapters of which tell the story of European conquest, several centuries of occupation, the subordination of the indigenous people and their treatment as cheap labour. The brutality of the apartheid state is just one aspect of this history, albeit the worst. Throughout, the colonized population had to struggle for its most basic rights. Healing such a tormented society – transforming what had effectively been a labour camp policed by armed guards into a community at peace with itself – is difficult and has taken and is still taking time.[71] The *ubuntu* discourse for reconciliation was a tool that alone was never going to be up to the task.

In his recent book, Premesh Lalu analyzes the TRC as a version of performative politics in which ideas of truth and reconciliation orbit in an endless spiral of imaginary solutions. In referring to it in terms of slapstick, he draws on the play *Ubu and the Truth Commission* written by aesthetics professor Jane Taylor and directed by artist, draughtsman and filmmaker William Kentridge, in which the ridiculous, grotesque figure of Ubu makes it seem like the TRC was a farce after the tragedy of Apartheid, leaving the spectator with the "troubling uncertainty of not knowing whether to laugh or cry."[72] The TRC was in the view of Lalu more than "an archive recalling the tragic consequences of the violence of apartheid." However, "recoiling from the horror of scenes of mutilation, murder and massacre," it ruled out an attitude towards slapstick and thus spontaneously emphasized "*affect* as necessary for recrafting freedom."[73] However, emotions with the aim of just forgiving, forgetting, and moving on meant repression of the past (in the sense of Freud) rather than coming to terms with it.

The vision of undoing apartheid provoked new ways of looking at concepts such as freedom, education, and race. Mandela's vision of a post-apartheid society that was free, democratic, and harmonious, that transcended race discrimination and was underpinned by the *ubuntu* discourse, mobilized the new nation. However, after him, the vision of undoing apartheid through a new race-transcending vocabulary became the undoing of his race-transcending freedom. The new market-radical definition of freedom was inconsistent with his vision of how to unpick apartheid. The neoliberal mantra defined freedom in ways that confronted his understanding of it, which was the harmonious cohabitation of whites and blacks. Neoliberal freedom was all about the market rights of the powerful, and it exacerbated race divisions by adding a class dimension to them.

In *Undoing Apartheid*, Lalu refers to the way the Nazi regime ended. The TRC's rationality, in Lalu's view, was "pitted against apartheid's enforced peace, rather than reflecting the post-World War II Nuremberg model, as is all too commonly believed in the familiar laying out of a miraculous triumph of redemption over retribution."[74] Lalu is right. Neither the fall of the apartheid nor the Nazi regime entirely managed to bring about redemption and avoid all retribution. Nuremberg was all about forgetting and moving on, rather than the post-apartheid version, which was all about forgiving and moving on, and this shows that there was a difference between the end of the apartheid and Nazi regimes. Apartheid's enforced peace didn't reflect the post-World War II model, a fact which showed itself later in various circumstances.

In the post-war German foundation myth in the years after 1945, with the execution of the Nazi leaders branded a band of criminals that had led their innocent people astray, redemption might have been in the minds of the victors (the allied governments who rearmed the two Germanies in return for their support in the Cold War), but within West Germany, the emphasis was on forgetting rather than forgiving. The Nuremberg trial sealed a pact of silence intended to conceal the Holocaust, and the silence lasted until the 1968 protests took place. (East Germany developed its particular form of forgetting by arguing that the Nazi regime was a consequence of capitalism which had its post-war representation in West Germany and had nothing to do with East Germany.)

Of course, since apartheid had imploded so publicly, concealing, and forgetting it was not an option for the TRC. Instead of forgetting and moving on, as in the German case, the slogan in South Africa was *forgiving* and moving on. However, the implicit rather than explicit idea within the *ubuntu* discourse was that it was not only about forgiving and moving on but, additionally, it should be accompanied by a social and economic program designed to confront racial inequalities. Such a program was not directly included in the *ubuntu* concept, though in hindsight, it is clear that the concept needed this support for sustainable credibility, and initially after 1994, there was awareness about this connection and steps were taken to establish it. The initially serious attempts to combine anti-racism with an expansive social program supporting education, health, and housing, lost impetus when social expansion was replaced by neoliberal market expansion and Mandela's race-transcending definition of freedom by neoliberal market freedom. Without the aid of a political and institutional infrastructure to assist redistribution and bridge the gap between differences of race and class, *ubuntu* ended prematurely, before it had the chance to gain *ujamaa's* ultimately iconic-nostalgic status. On this point, one finds a major reason of ubuntu's failure to lay the ghosts of apartheid to rest.

This view on the South African case has global relevance. Race-based discrimination compounded by class divisions exists worldwide with a variety of names, just as there are many forms of modern slavery and cases where freedom is subjugated to profit. In fact, the term 'freedom' has become a matter of race and class internationally. Of course, class here does not carry the strict Marxist meaning but should be understood as social stratification with an ever-growing group of unorganized workers at the bottom – those willing or obliged to migrate anywhere to do anything.

Confronting this development requires more than talk of a meta-norm and language about reconciliation. It would require a global economic-political program to fight poverty and create a fairer distribution of the Earth's resources. Such a program would have to be accompanied by institutions and a distinct normative scaffold constructed below the meta level to ensure relevance to people's everyday experiences. The institutions and norms created, and the policies and politics being made by them, would provide new points of departure for reconciliation, and not just gloss over past experiences of injustice. 'Forgiving and moving on' requires a broad social program. Attempts to create such a thing in South Africa declined after Mandela's departure.

On this point, a comparison with the *ujamaa* case is instructive. In Tanzania only rudimentary institutions existed to implement Nyerere's project, although, unlike in the South African *ubuntu* case, there was a clear vision of a new political economy. However, both the vision of national self-reliance in Tanzania and the race-transcending definition of freedom in Mandela's South Africa were at odds with the market radical globalization agenda which imposed austerity which in turn undermined the capacity for public welfare.

Certainly, the problem of corruption existed in both Tanzania and South Africa. However, one must remember that corruption was (and is) inherent in the practices of what was called the neoliberal approach, too, with its concentration of capital, insane wealth, and prospering offshore tax havens. Norms, institutions, and practices for the internationally coordinated political control of global capital and for redistributive planetary politics need to include the check of corruption at all levels.

Notes

1 Christian B. N. Gade, 'What is Ubuntu? Different Interpretations among the South Africans of African Descent,' *South African Journal of Philosophy* 31(33), 2012: 484–503; Christian B. N. Gade, 'The Historical Development of the Written Discourses on Ubuntu,' *South African Journal of Philosophy* 30(3), 2011: 303–29; Christian B. N.

1. Gade, *A Discourse on African Philosophy: A New Perspective on Ubuntu and Transitional Justice in South Africa*. (Lanham, MD: Lexington, 2017).
2. Gade, 'What is Ubuntu?'
3. Their role was much more ambiguous, with missionary allegiances often stretched between conflicting interests. Cf. Norman Etherington, 'Introduction,' in *Missions and Empire*, ed. Norman Etherington (Oxford: Oxford University Press, 2005), 1–18.
4. Etherington, 'Introduction,' 6.
5. Nigel Penn, *The Forgotten Frontier: Colonist & Khoisan on the Cape's Northern Frontier in the 18th Century* (Cape Town: Double Storey Books, 2005).
6. Penn, *Forgotten Frontier*, 6.
7. Richard Price, *Making Empire: Colonial Encounters and the Creation of Imperial Rule in Nineteenth-Century Africa* (Cambridge: Cambridge University Press, 2008).
8. Price, *Making Empire*, 1–2.
9. Etherington, 'Introduction,' 7. See also Peggy Brock, 'New Christians as Evangelists,' in *Missions and Empire*, ed. Norman Etherington (Oxford: Oxford University Press, 2005), 132–52.
10. Paul Landau, 'Language,' in *Missions and Empire*, ed. Norman Etherington (Oxford: Oxford University Press, 2005), 194–215.
11. Robert Moffat, *Missionary Labours and Scenes in Southern Africa* (London: John Snow, Paternoster-Row, 1842), 125.
12. Ibid., 225.
13. Ibid., 127.
14. Richard Elphick and Rodney Davenport (eds), *Christianity in South Africa: A Political, Social, and Cultural History* (Berkeley: University of California Press, 1997).
15. For the mission stations, see Ingie Hovland, *Mission Station Christianity: Norwegian Missionaries in Colonial Natal and Zululand, Southern Africa 1850–1890* (Leiden: Brill, 2013).
16. Richard Elphick, *The Equality of Believers: Protestant Missionaries and the Racial Politics of South Africa* (Charlottesville: University of Virginia Press, 2012), 18. For the mission stations, see also Hovland, *Mission Station Christianity*.
17. Elphick, *Equality of Believers*, 18.
18. Ibid., 18–19.
19. Ibid., 19.
20. Ibid., 25, 27.
21. Etherington, 'Introduction,' 10.
22. Hovland, *Mission Station Christianity*, 48, who builds on Axel-Ivar Berglund, *Zulu Thought-Patterns and Symbolism* (London: Hurst & Co., 1976) and Amanda Porterfield, 'The Impact of Early New England Missionaries on Women's Role in Zulu Culture,' *Church History* 66(1), 1997: 67–80.
23. Retief Müller, 'Afrikaner Missionaries and the Slippery Slope of Praying for Rain,' *Exchange* 46(1), 2017: 29–45.
24. Moffat, *Missionary Labours and Scenes*, 305, 314, 320, 325.
25. Hovland, *Mission Station Christianity*, 49–50; Berglund, *Zulu Thought-Patterns*, 248.
26. Hovland, *Mission Station Christianity*, 51–52.
27. Landau, 'Language,' 212.
28. Ibid., 210–12.
29. Hovland, *Mission Station Christianity*, 54.
30. Moffat, *Missionary Labours and Scenes*, 384.
31. Ibid., 402.
32. Lamin Sanneh, *Translating the Message: The Missionary Impact on Culture* (New York: Orbis, 1989), 53, quoted from Hovland, *Mission Station Christianity*, 56.
33. Müller, 'Afrikaner Missionaries,' 32–33.
34. Landau, 'Language,' 213.
35. I am most grateful to Ntozakhe Cezula for help with the Xhosa translation.

36 Jenifer M. Henderson, *The Musical Life of Henry Hare Dugmore, 1820 Settler*. Unpublished Master's Thesis, Rhodes University 1973, http://contentpro.seals.ac.za; Ivan Mitford-Barberton and Violet White, *Some Frontier Families: Biographical Sketches of 100 Eastern Province Families before 1840* (Cape Town: Human and Rousseau, 1969).
37 Landau, 'Language,' 211. Moffat, born in Scotland in 1795, moved to England to find work as a gardener and a farmer. Moffat, *Missionary Labours and Scenes*, 616–17; Thomas Fowell Buxton, *The African Slave Trade and Its Remedy* (London: J. Murray, 1839).
38 E. H. Crouch, *Life of Rev. H. H. Dugmore, Poet Preacher 1810–1897* (Grahamstown: Grocott & Sherry, 1920), 92–94. Cf. Henderson, 'Life of Henry Hare Dugmore,' 12.
39 Henderson, 'Life of Henry Hare Dugmore,' 64.
40 Literal translation: 'another Ubun'.
41 I am most grateful to Jacob Moikanyang for help with the Tswana translations.
42 John Whittley Appleyard, *The Kafir Language* (Graham's Town: Wesleyan Mission Society, 1850). Cf. Gade, 'Historical Development,' 307.
43 Appleyard, *The Kafir Language*, 106.
44 John William Colenso, *Elementary Grammar of the Zulu-Kafir Language: Prepared for the Use of Missionaries, and Other Students* (London: Richard Clay, 1855), 7, 14.
45 Colenso, *Elementary Grammar*, 15, 16.
46 Ibid., 18.
47 Ibid., 22.
48 John William Colenso, *Zulu–English Dictionary* (Pietermaritzburg: P. Davis, 1861), 353–54.
49 Bishop Colenso and Lewis Grout, *Tracts of Bishop Calenso and an American missionary (Rev. Lewis Grout) on the treatment of polygamy in converts from heathenism*. First published at Pietermaritzburg, Natal, in 1855, 1856. New Haven: New Englander 1858.
50 Jeff Guy, *The Heretic: A Study of the Life of John William Colenso, 1814–1883* (Johannesburg: Ravan Press, 1983).
51 Gade, 'Historical Development,' 307–308.
52 Gade, 'What is Ubuntu?' 488. Archibald Campbell Jordan's articles were republished in the book *Towards an African Literature: The Emergence of Literary Form in Xhosa* (Berkeley: University of California Press, 1973). Quoted here from Gade, 'What is Ubuntu?' 488.
53 Cited in Michael Onyebuchi Eze, *Intellectual History in Contemporary South Africa* (London: Palgrave, 2010), 103.
54 Stanlake Samkange and Tommie Marie Samkange, *Hunhuism or Ubuntuism: A Zimbabwe Indigenous Political Philosophy* (Salisbury: Graham Publishers, 1980).
55 See publications from the 'Ubuntu Project' launched by Drucilla Cornell at the Stellenbosch Institute for Advanced Study in 2003, in particular Drucilla Cornell and Nyoko Muvangua (eds), *uBuntu and the Law: African Ideals and Postapartheid Jurisprudence* (New York: Fordham University Press, 2012) and Drucilla Cornell and Karin van Marle, with Albie Sachs, *Albie Sachs and the Transformation in South Africa: From Revolutionary Activist to Constitutional Court Judge* (New York: Birkbeck Law Press, 2014).
56 Tom Bennett, *Ubuntu. An African Jurisprudence* (Cape Town: Juta & Company Ltd., 2018).
57 Ibid., 4–6.
58 Ibid., 27–28.
59 Ibid., 31–32.
60 For the theological perspective, see Kwasi Wiredu, *The Politics of Truth and Reconciliation in South Africa: Legitimizing the Post-apartheid State* (Cambridge: Cambridge University Press, 2001) and Kwasi Wiredu, *Cultural Universals and Particulars: An African Perspective* (Bloomington: Indiana University Press, 1996). For the emphasis of the difference between *ubuntu* and the Kantian concept of dignity, see Thaddeus Metz,

'Toward an African Moral Theory,' *Journal of Political Philosophy* 15(3), 2007: 321–41 and, less categorically, Laurie Ackermann, *Human Dignity: Lodestar for Equality in South Africa* (Cape Town: Juta, 2012) and Drucilla Cornell, 'Introduction: Transitional Justice versus Substantive Revolution,' in *Law and Revolution in South Africa: UBuntu, Dignity, and the Struggle for Constitutional Transformation*, ed. Drucilla Cornell (New York: Fordham University Press, 2014). See also for this discussion Bennett, *Ubuntu*, ch. 3.
61 Bennett, *Ubuntu*, 160–61.
62 Ibid., 162.
63 Ibid., 165.
64 Jeremy Seekings and Nicoli Nattrass, *Policy, Politics and Poverty in South Africa* (Basingstoke: Palgrave, 2015). See also Hein Marais, *South Africa Pushed to the Limit: The Political Economy of Change* (London: Zed, 2011).
65 James Ferguson, *Give a Man a Fish: Reflections on the New Politics of Distribution* (Durham, NC: Duke University Press, 2015).
66 Ferguson, *Give a Man a Fish*, 4–5.
67 Ibid., 5.
68 Ibid., 5.
69 Seekings and Nattrass, *Policy, Politics and Poverty*, 9.
70 Ibid., 10.
71 See here John S. Saul and Patrick Bond, *South Africa. The Present as History: From Mrs Ples to Mandela & Marikana* (Johannesburg: Jacana, 2014).
72 Premesh Lalu, *Undoing Apartheid* (Cambridge: Polity Press, 2023). The quotation on p. 139.
73 Ibid., 145.
74 Ibid., 174.

References

Ackermann, Laurie. *Human Dignity: Lodestar for equality in South Africa*. Cape Town: Juta, 2012.
Appleyard, John Whittley. *The Kafir Language*. Graham's Town: Wesleyan Mission Society, 1850.
Bennett, Tom. *Ubuntu. An African Jurisprudence*. Cape Town: Juta & Company Ltd., 2018.
Berglund, Axel-Ivar. *Zulu Thought-Patterns and Symbolism*. London: Hurst & Co., 1976.
Brock, Peggy. "New Christians as Evangelists." In *Missions and Empire*, edited by Norman Etherington, 132–52. Oxford: Oxford University Press, 2005.
Buxton, Thomas Fowell. *The African Slave Trade and Its Remedy*. London: J. Murray, 1839.
Colenso, Bishop and Lewis Grout, *Tracts of Bishop Calenso and an American missionary (Rev. Lewis Grout) on the treatment of polygamy in converts from heathenism*. First published at Pietermaritzburg, Natal, in 1855, 1856. New Haven: New Englander, 1858.
Colenso, John William. *Elementary Grammar of the Zulu-Kafir Language: Prepared for the Use of Missionaries, and Other Students*. London: Richard Clay, 1855.
———. *Zulu–English Dictionary*. Pietermaritzburg: P. Davis, 1861.
Colenso, John William and Rev. Lewis Grout. "Tracts of Bishop Colenso and an American Missionary (Rev. Lewis Grout) on the Treatment of Polygamy in Converts from Heathenism." *New Englander* XIV, no. 2 (1856): 407–433.
Cornell, Drucilla. "Introduction: transitional justice versus substantive revolution." *Law and Revolution in South Africa: Ubuntu, Dignity, and the Struggle for Constitutional Transformation*, edited by Drucilla Cornell, 1–18. New York: Fordham University Press, 2014.

Cornell, Drucilla and Nyoko Muvangua, eds. *uBuntu and the Law: African Ideals and Post-apartheid Jurisprudence*. New York: Fordham University Press, 2012.
Cornell, Drucilla and Karin van Marle, with Albie Sachs. *Albie Sachs and the Transformation in South Africa: From Revolutionary Activist to Constitutional Court Judge*. New York: Birkbeck Law Press, 2014.
Crouch, E. H. *Life of Rev. H. H. Dugmore, Poet Preacher 1810–1897*. Grahamstown: Grocott & Sherry, 1920.
Elphick, Richard. *The Equality of Believers: Protestant Missionaries and the Racial Politics of South Africa*. Charlottesville: University of Virginia Press, 2012.
Elphick, Richard and Rodney Davenport, eds. *Christianity in South Africa: A Political, Social, and Cultural History*. Berkeley: University of California Press, 1997.
Etherington, Norman. Introduction to *Missions and Empire*, 1–18, edited by Norman Etherington. Oxford: Oxford University Press, 2005.
Eze, Michael Onyebuchi. *Intellectual History in Contemporary South Africa*. London: Palgrave, 2010.
Ferguson, James. *Give a Man a Fish: Reflections on the New Politics of Distribution*. Durham, NC: Duke University Press, 2015.
Gade, Christian B. N. *A Discourse on African Philosophy: A New Perspective on Ubuntu and Transitional Justice in South Africa*. Lanham, MD: Lexington Books, 2017.
———. 'The Historical Development of the Written Discourses on Ubuntu.' *South African Journal of Philosophy* 30, no. 3 (2011): 303–29.
———. "What is Ubuntu? Different Interpretations among the South Africans of African Descent." *South African Journal of Philosophy* 31, no. 33 (2012): 484–503.
Guy, Jeff. The Heretic: *A Study of the Life of John William Colenso, 1814–1883*. Johannesburg: Ravan Press, 1983.
Henderson, Jenifer M. "The Musical Life of Henry Hare Dugmore, 1820 Settler." Unpublished Master's Thesis, Rhodes University, 1973. http://contentpro.seals.ac.za.
Hovland, Ingie. *Mission Station Christianity: Norwegian Missionaries in Colonial Natal and Zululand, Southern Africa 1850–1890*. Leiden: Brill, 2013.
Jordan, Archibald Campbell. *Towards an African Literature: The Emergence of Literary Form in Xhosa*. Berkeley: University of California Press, 1973.
Lalu, Premesh. *Undoing Apartheid*. Cambridge: Polity Press, 2023.
Landau, Paul. "Language." In *Missions and Empire*, edited by Norman Etherington, 194–215. Oxford: Oxford University Press, 2005.
Marais, Hein. *South Africa Pushed to the Limit: The Political Economy of Change*. London: Zed, 2011.
Metz, Thaddeus. "Toward an African Moral Theory." *Journal of Political Philosophy* 15, no. 3 (2007): 321–41.
Mitford-Barberton, Ivan and Violet White. *Some Frontier Families: Biographical Sketches of 100 Eastern Province Families before 1840*. Cape Town: Human and Rousseau, 1969.
Moffat, Robert. *Missionary Labours and Scenes in Southern Africa*. London: John Snow, Paternoster-Row, 1842.
Müller, Retief. "Afrikaner Missionaries and the Slippery Slope of Praying for Rain." *Exchange* 46, no. 1 (2017): 29–45. https://doi.org/10.1163/1572543X-12341429.
Penn, Nigel. *The Forgotten Frontier: Colonist & Khoisan on the Cape's Northern Frontier in the 18th Century*. Cape Town: Double Storey Books, 2005.
Porterfield, Amanda. "The Impact of Early New England Missionaries on Women's role in Zulu Culture." *Church History* 66, no. 1 (1997): 67–80.

Price, Richard. *Making Empire: Colonial Encounters and the Creation of Imperial Rule in Nineteenth-Century Africa*. Cambridge: Cambridge University Press, 2008.
Samkange, Stanlake and Tommie Marie Samkange. *Hunhuism or Ubuntuism: A Zimbabwe Indigenous Political Philosophy.* Salisbury: Graham Publishers, 1980.
Sanneh, Lamin. *Translating the Message: The Missionary Impact on Culture*. New York: Orbis, 1989.
Saul, John S. and Patrick Bond. *South Africa. The Present as History: From Mrs Ples to Mandela & Marikana*. Johannesburg: Jacana, 2014.
Seekings, Jeremy and Nicoli Nattrass. *Policy, Politics and Poverty in South Africa*. Basingstoke: Palgrave, 2015.
Wiredu, Kwasi. *Cultural Universals and Particulars: An African perspective*. Bloomington: Indiana University Press, 1996.
———. *The Politics of Truth and Reconciliation in South Africa: Legitimizing the Post-apartheid State*. Cambridge: Cambridge University Press, 2001.

Epilogue
Can we learn from *ujamaa* and *ubuntu*?

Why did the visions of *ujamaa* and *ubuntu* ultimately fail? And can we learn anything from their failure? In answering those questions, it is instructive to revisit Willy Brandt's North/South Commission and the work it did between 1977 and 1983 on a new world order. The commission was initiated by the World Bank as a think-tank tasked with finding ways to extinguish world poverty and the means to level North/South inequality. The Brandt Commission's work in the 1970s coincided with the collapse of the Western post-war dollar-centric economic world order. The collapse triggered a major push by the Third World (which is what the Global South was called at that time) to establish a New International Economic Order (NIEO). Within the United Nations Conference on Trade and Development, the 77 states representing the Third World were organized as the G77, and with the NIEO, their goal was a fairer distribution of the Earth's resources. They felt confident that it was their time to shine, but the instinctive reaction by the political leaders of the Transatlantic North was to ward off what they perceived as an attack on their old world order which, in today's retrospective view, had just collapsed To that purpose, they formed what later became the G7 to confront and dilute the claims of the G77. However, the situation was not quite as black and white as that, and many in the North considered the South's claims justified and fair. Siding with this minority view, the Brandt Commission proposed a new world order based on the G77's NIEO.[1]

The histories of *ujamaa* and *ubuntu*, as well as the Brandt Commission, all expose the gap between normative power on the one hand and economic and political power on the other. They point to the chasm that lies between visions and dreams of a better future and the political and economic power necessary to realize them. All three ideas had discursive power, which gave them political power, but it was not enough to control economic power. The Brandt Commission had a much more elaborate idea of institutions and rules required for the implementation of its one-world vision of a redistributive, political world economy than the *ujamaa* project had about how to realize its vision. The latter certainly possessed a clear vision of an agrarian economy that would provide national self-reliance through a web of village communities, but it was vague about how that vision would be implemented. The *ubuntu* discourse dealt with a post-apartheid meta-norm of reconciliation, forgiveness, and moving on. Although the new post-apartheid government was aware of the need for expansive social policies, it failed to carry them out, and, anyway, the awareness of the need was not expressed in the *ubuntu* discourse.

The Brandt Commission's proposal and the *ujamaa* project were introduced during a highly transformative period in which a paradigmatic shift took place from Keynesian ideas of political management of the economy to the market-radical escape from political management that, in the 1990s, came to be called neoliberal globalization. One might describe the transformation as one in which capitalism escaped the position it had been assigned to since 1945 and was set free from being embedded at the national level to enjoy unrestrained global movements of capital, commodities, and labour. The *ubuntu* discourse coincided with the break-through of the new approach that emerged in response to the 1970s crisis, the break-through of the neoliberal argument that politics should steer clear of market interventions. One might even say that the *ubuntu* discourse was absorbed by the triumphing neoliberalism with its end-of-history euphoria. By then neoliberal practices had adopted a laissez-faire approach.

Although the Brandt Commission supported monitoring the economy globally and proposed international taxes as a tool for redistribution, its weakness was that it circumvented the question of how global corporations could be controlled and what post-Fordist capitalism meant. For instance, its proposal for international taxes did not cover corporations. Not dissimilarly, the *ujamaa* project was based on the illusion that global corporations could be nationalized by a national government without intergovernmental coordination. Of course, when Nyerere launched the project in 1967, few had the foresight to realize that a major shift towards the transnationalization of economic power (which would circumvent national political control) was about to occur.

The lesson of all these projects is that visions and meta-norms require institutions and political action for their implementation. Neither visions nor their underlying concepts achieve anything alone. Euphoria alone does not mean implementation. Another lesson is that national economies are too small to monitor and manage redistributive politics and that therefore there is a need for global monitoring and the coordination of the world's economy through the synergy of improved norms, institutions, and policies. The issue of capitalism's border-transcending power needs to be addressed not shirked. A global political economy requires not only a global market but also politics that transcend national borders, monitoring and managing the global market and its powerful agents from a social and redistributive perspective. There was a deficit on this point that had impact on the preconditions to realize both the *ujamaa* and the *ubuntu* goals.

Here one must add that politically managing the global market does not mean dreams of a world government but norms and institutions organizing and coordinating planetary cooperation in what Chakrabarty describes as the many worlds (Introduction). One might think of a reformed UN as a model. The shortcomings of the existing UN are well known and don't need to be repeated here. One might reflect on the vitality of the UN around the NIEO in the 1970s asking why it failed and what we can learn from the failure. This conclusion is obvious also in the assessment of the Brandt Commission and its unspoken circumvention of global corporations.

The *ujamaa* and *ubuntu* cases show that the national framework was too narrow for sustainable success. Against advancing neoliberal power, national politics was quite helpless. The problem with *ubuntu* was not the national framework per se, but its lack with a link to political economy with a social profile and for such a political economy the national framework was too narrow.

Politically powerful concepts, such as *ujamaa* and *ubuntu*, full as they necessarily are of ambiguity and contradiction, are hard to pin down. Inviting a variety of interpretations, they defy any simple clear, precise definition. The struggle to give meaning to key concepts such as those, is the core of politics. Nietzsche described this condition by saying that concepts that can be defined have no history. Having a history means being ambiguous. The ambiguity is thus not a problem but the point of departure for discursive struggles about interpretation and meaning.

Translations increase the ambiguity. There is a political potential in the ambiguity through translations, as Benjamin reminded us in the Introduction: mimesis, the principle of imitation, is a source of richness, because it is a source of thinking in terms of alternatives. The target is as the Introduction argued not sameness and identity but understanding difference. Both *ujamaa* and *ubuntu* contribute to a planetary understanding of difference.

A greater understanding of difference would, as the Introduction argued, be a major achievement in the work for a new conceptualization of the world. A planetary understanding of difference would be the basis for inclusive planetary visions and the policies necessary for their implementation (with the term planetary as defined by the Introduction). The early missionaries' ambition to convert the indigenous people, when, in what is today South Africa, they found *ubuntu* while searching for a language that could describe *their* religious experience, is not a useful point of reference anymore. The issue at stake is not about converting to sameness but understanding difference. The planetary perspective should emerge through an intellectual exchange of experiences and values, taking and giving, learning and understanding, rather than teaching and proclaiming. The exploration of *ujamaa* and *ubuntu* shows how, through translation, concepts such as these can be a crucial tool in the development of a global approach to the understanding of difference and, on that basis, promote questions about what is shared and what is not. Understanding of difference and of the Other must underpin the search for common ground, common norms, and institutions. This argument is certainly meta-normative, and even if it is far from congruent with existing practices, will nevertheless be vital in our debate on alternative futures.

Understanding difference connects the planetary perspective to the reality of the many worlds, to use Chakrabarty's dichotomy. Understanding difference is not the goal but the point of departure for the Kantian non-utopian work on a better world. One might say that this argument is wishful thinking and expresses delirious desires without substance. However, one might also say that the planet's condition and the declining prospects of long-term survival of the species *homo sapiens* necessitates it. On this point, one might refer to Latour's despairing sigh, rather than encouraging optimism, before he departed (Introduction).

Can we learn from history? Nobody emphasized more than Nietzsche that humans are condemned to repeat their disastrous and ill-fated mistakes. They never learn from them. From a more epistemological perspective than Nietzsche's philosophical one, one could echo him by arguing that history never precisely reiterates itself, because even if there are reiterating elements and structures, they occur in new contexts, never exactly as they were. So, in the sense that every situation is new to a smaller or greater degree, we cannot learn from the past.

However, this pessimistic view must not go unchallenged, even if its core is undeniable. Other views on the past emphasize history as a learning process, enforcing us to come to terms with our experiences and giving us a chance to learn from them. Reinhart Koselleck, quoted in the Introduction, distinguished between the experiences of history's losers and winners, arguing that the losers had more reason to reflect on their situation than the winners. Learning from mistakes in the past meant reflecting on how they could be avoided in the future. The winners took their situation for granted without any further reflection or ambition of learning from the past. The problem for the losers, however, is that their experiences are continually connected to new experiences in such a way that makes it difficult for them over a longer period of time (two-three generations) to accurately remember the old experiences and translate them into an action plan for the future. After two or three generations, the memory of the experience fades, and the filter of continuously new contexts dilutes it. This circumstance is a factor to consider but not an obstacle when reflecting on why a project failed and trying to learn from it.

A way of ameliorating our human condition and responding to our difficulty in learning from the past might be to interpret learning less instrumentally, more creatively. Reflecting on the past, particularly on lost opportunities and failures, opens one's eyes to alternatives in history, to opportunities that were not fulfilled, and invites one to reflect on why they were missed. Other questions raised by such reflection include whether the opportunities could be revised and updated or where the alternatives are in the present and how they could be approached. In this way, the past could be a source of inspiration and positively impact our own time and situation.

A new planetary understanding of difference, as the Introduction laid it out, does not argue that a new universalism should follow the failures of neoliberal globalization. Reinhart Koselleck's approach to conceptual history is a source of inspiration for this short book, as is his work on a theory of historical time in which he reflects on the two world wars, various global economic crises, the Cold War's nuclear balance of terror and the ecological crisis. He uncovers the teleology of the enlightenment project and its ideologies – communism, liberalism, socialism, and nationalism – which saw history as inherently bound towards a predetermined goal, which, in their secularized versions of the Christian eschatology, was only achievable after a final climactic crisis (the hypocrisis that is triggered by hypocrisy). He looks for a history of alternatives, the (never realized) possibilities in history, history in the plural, which doesn't have a reason, or a cunning as Hegel believed.

As the Introduction outlined, instead of spouting utopian futures which are derived from historical reason and achieved through apocalyptic transitions, Koselleck searched empirically rather than theoretically for alternatives that would emerge in the gap between experiences and expectations, which too often became a gap between expectations and disappointment. The deep empiricism of his thinking on the continuous revision of the past and the future, in a kind of learning process, where the learning has a limited duration, was not very optimistic, and he warned not only of new ahistorical utopias propelling man towards a predetermined goal, but also that the day might come when the experiences of disappoint become so great that the capacity to outline new expectations is exhausted.[2] Even so, he insisted that the future remains open and unpredictable, which also leaves room for hope, whether big or small. This thought provokes action because it makes clear that humans have their futures (in the plural) in their own hands. There are several ways the future could be shaped. Koselleck shows how planetary cohabitation could be built with empiricism and experiences rather than utopia, bottom up rather than top down, Kant rather than Hegel. *Ujamaa* and *ubuntu* recall another of Koselleck's arguments, that history's losers learn more about how to cope with the future than its winners. In a time of crisis, with growing social fractures within and between nations, his reflection on the conditions of possible histories, on alternative histories, becomes urgent.

The point is not to construct a new revolutionary utopia of eternal planetary peace, but pragmatically to build new communities beyond nation states which have the capacity to respond to the big challenges of our time, of which the biggest is the fact that it is digitized nanosecond-driven unrestrained capitalism that is the allocator of scarce global resources. The governments seem to have reduced their roles to legitimize this development. There is a need for a new understanding of the relationship between resource-coordinating and resource-distributing politics and border-transcending capitalism. The conceptualization for the planetary perspective we are looking for should not be conceived as a multicultural add-on to the Eurocentric modernization perspective through indigenous cultures and languages. The search should be for the 'in-betweens' within cultures and nations and unions of nations, such as the African Union and the European Union, and for the conceptual borderlands transcending the borders, the conceptual overlaps connecting differences and the in-betweens of the approximations in translations. Benoît Challand and Chiara Bottici refer to the interstices between nations and cultures in their argument for an interstitial global critical theory and use a metaphorical musical language to illustrate what they mean. They quote jazz musician Miles Davis ("don't play what is there, play what is not there") and Claude Debussy's definition of music as "the space between the notes."[3] On that basis, the task is to conceptualize moderating, regulating redistributive politics for peaceful planetary cohabitation; *ujamaa* and *ubuntu* politics, as opposed both to the politics of economic laissez-faire and xenophobic nationalism.

The understanding of difference might also imply learning from it. One thing that connects the *ujamaa* and the *ubuntu* discourses, but distinguishes them from the West, is the relationship between community and individuals. In mainstream

European philosophy, community is derived from the individual. Community is an aggregate of individuals. The focus is on the individual in expressions like human dignity, human rights, and human values. In the concepts of *ubuntu* and *utu* (the latter of which provided a core dimension to *ujamaa*), it is not the I that constructs the We, but the We that constitute the I.[4] Hannah Arendt is as we saw an exceptional voice in Western philosophy on this subject, building a bridge to African philosophy, although she was probably unaware of the link herself.

The African pattern goes beyond Swahili and Xhosa. The Xhosa saying, *umuntu ngamuntu ngabantu* ("a person is a person through other people"), has corresponding expressions in other African languages. *Botho* is the Sotho* version of *ubuntu*. (*The language of the Bantu ethnizes in northern South Africa, Botswana, and Lesotho.) The corresponding phrase in this region is *motho ke motho ka batho*, meaning that to be a human being is to affirm one's humanity by recognizing the humanity of others, to establish human relations with them. In Zimbabwe, Samkange's *hunhuism*, referred to in the previous chapter, relies on the corresponding concept in Shona, *hunhu* or *unhu*, which has the same meaning. The founding president of Zambia, Kenneth Kaunda, integrated what he called African humanism into his state ideology, reinterpreting it in a distinctly socialist way.[5]

In African languages, the common denominator of these concepts of humanism is the primacy of a normative definition of humanity: being human means having social and moral attributes. Biological definitions are absent or irrelevant. The focus is on human qualities and interactions in an anthropocentric philosophy, and it transcends a focus on humans as individuals.[6]

At first glance one might think that there are strong connections between this African philosophy and ethical principles in Christendom (cf. Sermon on the Mount) or even in any other religion in which there exists the idea of 'what you want people to do for you, you must do for them.' However, this ethical norm is an individual action imperative. The responsibility for complying with it is with the individuals. Moreover, African philosophy that sees the human as part of a community is more about demonstrating an empirical fact than proposing a normative appeal.

Ultimately, the final facet of the work from a planetary perspective brings us back to Bruno Latour's despairing but powerful argument in the Introduction and deals with our conceptual tools. The story of *ujamaa* and *ubuntu* – and the Brandt Commission – deals with the capacity to come to terms with global capitalism. When we talk about establishing institutions and norms to politically control global capitalism, we cannot avoid a reference to Karl Polanyi. His *The Great Transformation* was written in response to the European crises that led to the Second World War. Towards the end of the war, he talks about the embedding and disembedding forces of governments and capitalism. Politics (or governments), and the political pressures they are exposed to, which drive politics, embed, while capitalism tries to disembed itself.[7] However, in the pure form Polanyi imagined, these categories do not exist. Politics (or governments) and political pressures represent capital as much as they monitor and control it. Didn't post-1980 radical market-liberal politics, which were adopted by governments in the North as well as the South, promote capital's escape from their political control, i.e., they were disembedding forces? The goal of capital's disembedding, not against politics but promoted by politics, is to subordinate everything – commodities, services, and labour – to market principles where everything is treated as a commodity. However, Polanyi argued, humans are unwilling to accept that they have become commodities. They will in the end, before they reach the status as commodities, resist, which in turn, will interrupt the process of disembedding, so embedding can begin again. However, isn't a considerable part of the global labour today treated like commodities? Aren't they in fact commodities? Even in his time, Marx thought that they were. However, he also imagined that being commodities, people would develop class consciousness which would help them confront their situation, and this doesn't seem relevant today. To a considerable degree, global capital has succeeded in the commodification of labour. Polanyi's seesaw doesn't function. The ends of the seesaw move up and down like Polanyi's disembedding and reembedding. However, capitalism is not at one of the seesaw's ends but constitutes its constant balance point. That is the big problem needed to articulate and confront. Polanyi's theory was path-breaking and is still thought-provoking, but it requires conceptual revision and updating. A different but related question: What does universal in universal human rights mean? Is it there just to remind us of an ideal which was never realized? It is indeed Latour's desire for a new Copernican conceptual revolution that should guide our shaping of the future. The (re)conceptualization is key. The stories of the ultimate failure of the *ujamaa* and *ubuntu* projects could inspire the work.

Notes

1 For an assessment of the Brandt Commission's proposal, see Bo Stråth, *The Brandt Commission and the Multinationals. Planetary Perspectives* (London: Routledge, 2023).
2 Reinhart Koselleck, *Kritik und Krise. Eine Studie zur Pathogenese der bürgerlichen Welt* (Frankfurt/Main: Suhrkamp, 1973 [1959]), English translation *Critique and Crisis. Enlightenment and the Pathogenesis of Modern Society* (Cambridge, MA: MIT Press, 2000 [1988]); Reinhart Koselleck, *Vergangene Zukunft. Zur Semantik geschichtlicher Zeiten* (Frankfurt/Main: Suhrkamp, 1979). English translation *Futures Past. On the Semantics of Historical Time* (New York: Columbia University Press, 2004); Reinhart Koselleck, *Zeitschichten. Studien zur Historik* (Frankfurt/Main: Suhrkamp, 2003). For a comprehensive outline of Koselleck's work, see Stefan-Ludwig Hoffmann, *Der Riss in der Zeit. Kosellecks ungeschriebene Historik* (Berlin: Suhrkamp, 2023).
3 Benoît Challand and Chiara Bottici, 'Toward an Interstitial Global Critical Theory,' *Globalizations* 2021: 1–23. DOI:10.1080/14747731.2021.1989140.
4 Alena Rettová, 'Cognates of *Ubuntu*: Humanity/Personhood in the Swahili Philosophy of *Utu*,' *Decolonial Subversions* 2020: 31–60.
5 Ibid., 34.
6 Ibid., 5–37.
7 Karl Polanyi, *The Great Transformation. The Political and Economic Origins of Our Time* (Boston, MA: Beacon Press, 1944).

References

Brunner, Otto, Werner Conze and Reinhart Koselleck. *Geschichtliche Grundbegriffe: Historisches Lexikon zur politisch-sozialen Sprache in Deutschland, Band 1-8/2*. Stuttgart: Klett-Cotta, 1972–1997.

Challand, Benoît and Chiara Bottici. "Toward an Interstitial Global Critical Theory." *Globalizations* (2021): 1–23. DOI: 10.1080/14747731.2021.1989140.

Hoffmann, Stefan-Ludwig. *Der Riss in der Zeit. Kosellecks ungeschriebene Historik*. Berlin: Suhrkamp, 2023.

Koselleck, Reinhart. *Kritik und Krise. Eine Studie zur Pathogenese der bürgerlichen Welt*. Frankfurt/Main: Suhrkamp 1973 [1959], English translation *Critique and Crisis. Enlightenment and the Pathogenesis of Modern Society*. Cambridge, MA: MIT Press, 2000 [1988].

———. *Vergangene Zukunft – Zur Semantik geschichtlicher Zeiten*. Frankfurt am Main: Suhrkamp, 1979. English translation *Futures Past. On the Semantics of Historical Time*. New York: Columbia University Press, 2004.

———. *Zeitschichten. Studien zur Historik*. Frankfurt/Main: Suhrkamp, 2003.

Polanyi, Karl. *The Great Transformation. The Political and Economic Origins of Our Time*. Boston, MA: Beacon Press, 1944.

Rettová, Alena. "Cognates of *Ubuntu*: Humanity/Personhood in the Swahili Philosophy of *Utu*." *Decolonial Subversions* (2020): 31–60.

Stråth, Bo. *The Brandt Commission and the Multinationals. Planetary Perspectives*. London: Routledge, 2023.

Index

Note: Page numbers followed by "n" refer to end notes.

African National Congress 77, 79, 83–6
African humanism 12, 21, 56–7, 76–7, 99; *ubuntu* translation 12
Africanization 24, 28, 81
agriculture 31–2, 43, 36; plantation economy 34
alienation 6, 8, 29; *see also* Arendt, H.; capitalism; Koselleck, R.
Amin, I. 36, 44
Angola 79
Aniara 6
Anthropocene 2, 5, 7
apartheid 12, 56, 67, 75–9, 83, 85–7; *see also* post-apartheid
Appleyard, J.W. 67–8, 71–4; and his translation of New Testament into Xhosa 68–9, 71–3
Arendt, H. 5–6, 8, 13, 99; *see also* alienation
artificial intelligence 6
Arusha Declaration 17–20, 22–4, 29–32, 34, 36; its heydays 17–18; Nsa-Kaisi 23; Scandinavian perspectives 40; *see also Uhuru*
Arusha Declaration Monument 25, 29, 33, 34–5
Arusha Declaration Museum 23
austerity 36–7, 41, 46, 85, 88

Bandung conference 2
Begriffsgeschichte 9
Benjamin, W. 9, 96; translation as juxtaposition 9
Berlin Missionary Society 62, 68
Besserwisser 18
Bible 12, 60–2, 64–5, 67; and Book of Jude 68; and Book of Mark 69–70; and Book of Revelations 69; and Martin Luther's New Testament 69; and the Book of Joshua 73; and the Old Testament 63–4, 68; and the Pentateuch 73; and the translation of the New Testament 57, 65, 67–73
Birmingham 67
Boipatong massacre 79
Botswana 56, 58, 99
Bottici, C 98
bottom-up 4, 18, 32–4, 37–9, 44–5
Boyce, W.B. 67; and his *Grammar of the Kaffir Language* 67
Brandt, W. 7, 47, 94; *see also* Brandt Commission
Brandt Commission 47, 94–6, 99; and G7 94; and G77 13, 47, 94
Bretton Woods 41, 45
Britain 11, 44, 58, 62, 64
British Kaffraria 67
Buthelezi, M. (Gatsha) 77
Buxton, T.F. 68

Cancún Summit 46–7
Cape Colony 57, 59–61, 67–8, 72; earlier name of Cape of Good Hope 57, 60; and its Eastern province 59
Cape Town 58–9, 82
capitalism 5, 12, 39, 49, 87, 95, 98, 99; *see also* globalization; industrialization; Keynesian economics; neoliberalism
Césaire, A. 2
Chakrabarty, D. 3, 6–8, 10, 48, 95; his monograph *Provincializing Europe* 2, 7–8, 13, 48

Index

Challand, B. 98
citizen 9, 29, 85; and the concept of citoyen 9; and the concept of *Staatsbürger* 9
civilizing mission 1, 28–9, 57
climate catastrophe 1, 5
cohabitation 2–3, 5, 10, 13, 79, 87, 98; *see also* planetary understanding
Cold War 2–3, 5, 19, 37, 41–5, 48, 79, 87, 97; as bipolar world 2, 19, 44; *see also* superpowers
Colenso, J.W. 63, 65–6, 74; *Elementary Grammar of the Zulu-Kafir Language: Prepared for the Use of Missionaries, and Other Students* 71; *and* his concept of polygamy 73; *and* his concept of polygenism 73; and his definition of *ubuntu* 71–3; and *Zulu-English dictionary* (1861) 71–2
Colonial Legislative Council 19
colonialism 1, 3, 19, 28, 40, 44–5, 57, 72, 78; colonized 37, 48, 64, 73, 86; colonizer 37, 48, 73; neocolonialism 10, 40, 46; postcolonialism 10, 19, 48; *see also* decolonization
Common Good Project 81
communism 37–8, 77, 85, 97; Chinese Maoist 11, 19 (*see also* Marxism); Stalinism 37; state controlled economy 36
conceptual history 9–10, 12, 18, 57, 71, 97; *see also Begriffsgeschichte*; Koselleck, R
Copernican Revolution 2, 100

Dar es Salaam 25, 30, 42, 47, 52n62; *see also* Arusha Declaration
Davenport, R. 62
Davis, M. 98
Davis, W. J. 68
Debussy, C. 98
decolonization 10, 12, 18, 22, 40, 42, 45–6, 48, 57, 83; *see also* colonization
Defiance Campaign 75
Döhne, J. 68
Drum Magazine 75, 78
Dugmore, H.H. 67–8, 70–4; and his translation of the New Testament into Xhosa 72–3
Durban 75, 80

Eastern Cape 59, 67, 71, 75; British Kaffraria 67
Eastern Cape Albany settlers 67
The Economic Freedom Fighters 86
Edinburgh 19
elections of 1994 79–80, 83, 86–7
Elphick, R. 62–3
enlightenment 1, 7, 8, 48, 48, 81, 97; and European Enlightenment 12–13, 31
Erlander, T. 41
Etherington, N 59, 64
ethnophilosophy 18, 48
exploitation 1, 3, 5, 9–10, 19, 25, 28; *see also unyonyaji*

The Fabian Society 19; *see also* socialism
Fabianism 11–12
Fanon, F. 48
forced villagization 32, 36
Foucault, M. 48
freedom *see Uhuru*
Freud, S. 5, 40, 87

Gade, C. 57, 67, 70–1, 75
Gandhi, M. 20; Phoenix Settlement 20; *see also* Nobel Prize
Genadendal 62
globalization 1, 4–6, 8, 42, 44, 46, 88, 95, 97; and the 19th-century Eurocentrism narrative 5; and the financial collapse of 2008 4; *see also* modernization; neoliberalism
Graham's Town 67; Grahamstown 59, 67
Griqua Town 68; Griekwasta 68
Growth, Employment and Redistribution (GEAR) 85

Hancock, K. 58
heathen beliefs 63, 65, 70, 73
Hegel, G.W.F. 8, 13, 97–8
Hountondji, P. 48
Hovland, I. 64
human rights 8, 30, 42, 44, 48, 82, 99, 100

Imvo Zabantsundu 75
industrialization 1, 29, 34; deindustrialization 85
Inkatha Freedom Party (IFP) 77, 79
Inkatha National Cultural Liberation Movement 77
International Monetary Fund (IMF) 36–7, 41–2, 45–6

Jordan, A.C. 75–6

kaDinuzulu, S. 77
Kaffir language 67; hate speech 67
Kagame, A. 75
Kant, I. 6, 8, 13, 81, 96, 98
Kaunda, K. 48, 78, 99
Kemp, J. van der 66
Kentridge, W. 86
Kenyatta, J. 48
Keynesian economics 44, 83, 95
Kilimanjaro 17, 23
kinship 19–20
Klerk, F. W. de 79
Koselleck, R. 4, 6, 9, 97–8; translation as juxtaposition 9
kujitegemea 24, 31–2, 38, 42
Kuruman 61, 68

Lalu, P. 86–7
Landau, P. 65, 70
Latour, B. 2–3, 97, 99, 100; new language 3
liberalism 7, 77, 97
lingua franca 8, 20, 60
London Missionary Society 66–7
Luthuli, A. 76

Makukula, D. 29, 34–5
Malema, J. 86
mamlaka 30
Mandela, N. 79–80, 85, 87–8; release from prison 79; *see also* Nobel Peace Prize
Marikana Massacre 86
Martinsson, H. 6
Marxism 6, 12, 20, 39, 88, 100
Mbeki, T. 85
Mbembe, A. 6, 10, 48
McNamara, R. 36
meta-norm 5, 8, 80, 88, 94–6; *ubuntu* as a meta-norm 88
Methodist 62, 67, 69, 72–3
mimesis 9, 96; *see also* Benjamin, W.
missionaries 21, 58–9, 62–5, 67, 70–5, 96; Christian missionaries 12, 56–60; and the meaning of *ubuntu* 65–74; and Manichean worldview 56, 64–5, 70, 72–3; missionary frontier 58
Mkpa, B.W. 42–3
modernity 2–3, 7, 10–11, 18, 29, 34
modernization 1–2, 7–8, 10, 28, 31–2, 48, 98; as paradigm 37, 40, 42

modimo 65–6; and the multiple meanings of 65
Moffat, R. 61, 64–8, 70, 73; *Moffat, Missionary Labours and Scenes* 68; and his translation of New Testament into Tswana 67–8, 70, 73
Moravian Brothers 62
Mpaka, B. 23
Mudimbe, V. 48
Mwinyi, A.H. 42
Mwongozo document 39, 42, 44–5

Namaqualand 68
Namibia 78
Natal 63, 65, 71–2, 77
nationalism 2–4, 7, 37, 77, 97; xenophobic nationalism 2–3, 5, 98
nationalization 24–5, 32, 95; of banks in Tanzania 24, 36; of companies in Tanzania 29, 36
neoliberalism 4, 18–19, 42, 44, 83–8, 95; anti-neoliberalism 83–4, 86
New International Economic Order (NIEO) 2, 10, 13, 45–7, 94–5
Nganang, P. 48
Ngubane, J.K. 75–6; *An African Explains Apartheid* 76; *Conflict of Minds* 76 (*see also* Drum Magazine); *Uvalo Lwezinhlonzi* 76
Nietzsche, F. 6, 96–7
Nkrumah, K. 21, 37, 48
Nobel Peace Prize: Klerk, F. W. de 79; Luthuli, A 76; Mandela, N. 79; Tuti, D. 82
North/South 7, 10, 46, 94; decolonization discourse 10; *see also* New International Economic Order; South Commission; Third World
Nsa-Kaisi 23
Nuremberg Trials 87
Nyerere, J. (K.) 11, 17–25, 29–4, 36–49, 88, 95; as *Mwalimu* 22–4, 29, 38, 43, 49; pamphlet in 1962 28; speech act moment 11, 22–7; speech in 1967 23–4; speech in Geneva 47; *see also* Arusha Declaration

one-party democracy 38

Palme, O. 41
Pan-Africanism 37, 42

Penn, N. 58
Piestist 60, 62, 69, 72–3
Pietermaritzburg 73
planetary understanding 8, 96–7
Polanyi, K. 99–100
Posselt, C.W. 68
post-apartheid 56, 79, 94–5; *ubuntu* in post-apartheid 83–5, 87
post-apocalypse 13
press 20, 24, 25, 27, 40; *The Daily News* 28; *The Standard* 24–5, 27; in Tanzania 20
Price, R. 59
privatization 43, 85
Promotion of National Unity and Reconciliation Act 81
Prussian Missionary Society 62

Reagan, R. 46
Reconstruction and Development Program (RDP) 83, 85
Revolution State Party 42
Riebeeck, Jan van 58
Rivonia Trial 79
Robben Island 79
Royal Geographic Society 68

Saïd, E. 48
salvation 63–4, 72
Samkange, S. 77–8, 99
Samkange, T.M. 77–8, 99
Scandinavia 40–1, 62
self-reliance *see kujitegemea*
semantic field 28, 42, 56–7, 69, 72; *ubuntu* in a semantic field 69
Senghor, L. 48; concept of *négritude* 48
Sermon on the Mount 99
Sharpeville Massacre 76, 86
Shivji, I. G. 32, 36, 42
Shutte, A. 81
Simensen, J. 40
socialism 7, 11, 19, 30, 77, 97, 99; early socialists 20; Fabian Society 19–21; *ujamaa* 11–12, 17, 19, 24–5, 42, 48, 57
Sokoine, E. M. 42
South Africa 10, 12, 20, 56, 58, 60, 62, 68, 70, 75–81, 83–8, 96, 99
South Commission 47; *see also* North/South Commission
Soviet Union 3, 5, 79

speech act theory 11, 24; *see also* Nyerere, J.
Sputnik 5–6
superpowers 42–5, 48
Swaziland (since 2018 Eswatini) 75

Tanganyika 19–20
Tanganyika African National Union (TANU) 11, 17, 19–20, 22–5, 28, 33; and *The Nationalist* 22–4, 27, 42; *see also* Mwongozo document; Revolution State Party; Youth League
TANU Conference in 1973 32–3
Tanzania 10–11, 17–20, 22–5, 29–33, 36–40, 42–7, 49, 57, 85, 88; media in Tanzania 25
Taylor, J. 86
Thatcher, M. 46
Third World 2, 10, 13, 41–2, 45–7, 94
Tönnies, F. 28–9
top-down 18, 32–4, 37, 39, 44–5
transcendentalism 13, 21, 71
Truth and Reconciliation Commission (TRC) 81–2; *see also* Tuti, D.
Tuti, D. 82
Tutsi Group 75

Uhuru 22–3, 28, 48–9
United Nations 4, 10, 13, 30, 45, 94, 95
United Nations Conference on Trade and Development 94
unyonyaji 28, 30, 32, 34, 41, 43, 45, 63
utopia 13, 21, 98

village community 11, 28, 30–2; and its contradictions 32; concept of *vijijini* 32–3; Groundnut Scheme 32 (*see also kujitegemea*); new elites 38; Operation Planned Villages 36

Wallerstein, I. 2–3, 7
Warner, J. 68
Weber, M. 8, 43
Wesleyan Missionary Society 67–8
World Bank 32, 36–7, 41–3, 45–8, 94

Youth League 22, 77, 86

Zambia 78, 99
Zanzibar 19–20, 42
Zuma, J. 85

For Product Safety Concerns and Information please contact our EU representative GPSR@taylorandfrancis.com
Taylor & Francis Verlag GmbH, Kaufingerstraße 24, 80331 München, Germany

www.ingramcontent.com/pod-product-compliance
Lightning Source LLC
Chambersburg PA
CBHW071823230426
43670CB00013B/2546